# THE RON JUKES STORY
# SUPER**SCOUT**

THE RON JUKES STORY
# SUPER**SCOUT**

RON JUKES WITH GEOFF ALLMAN

TEMPUS

'Of the many jobs within the football industry, scouting is probably the least glamorous and the least publicised. It is, however, without doubt one of the most important and masters of the art like Ron Jukes are worth their weight in gold.'

Brian Halford (*Birmingham Post and Mail* reporter)

First published 2006

Tempus Publishing Limited
The Mill, Brimscombe Port,
Stroud, Gloucestershire, GL5 2QG
www.tempus-publishing.com

British Library Cataloguing in Publication Data.
A catalogue record for this book is available from the British Library.

ISBN 0 7524 3070 X

Typesetting and origination by Tempus Publishing Limited
Printed in Great Britain

# CONTENTS

# INTRODUCTION

Lifelong friends Ron Jukes and Geoff Allman went to the same school (Queen Mary's Grammar School, Walsall), did the same holiday jobs at Walsall Inland Revenue when students and worked in education for many years (Ron as a head teacher, Geoff as a teacher trainer in a university). For over sixty years they have shared the same infatuation with football.

Ron as a scout and Geoff as a scribe with several books and many articles on the game fitted in their football activities alongside full-time jobs until Ron's retirement in 1985, when he became a full-time chief scout. For many years they talked of doing a book together on Ron's scouting career, but were then distracted. Finally, within two years of the start of a new millennium, they got down to what they thought was a manageable task. The more they worked at it, the more there seemed still to do.

Ill health and bereavements slowed the process down. It eventually became clear that, however long the book, there would still be some stories untold and some people not included. Here then are just a few of the adventures that have befallen Ron during his career in scouting. We hope that you get as much pleasure reading about them as we have done in writing about them.

Ron Jukes
Geoff Allman

# ACKNOWLEDGEMENTS

I should like to thank all the people who have helped me along the various stages of the journey. I owe so much to my 'childminder', Ivy Beavan, who first took me as a five-year-old to Walsall's former ground at Fellows Park. She sparked off my interest in both football and cricket and throughout her long life (1914–2000) she was the personification of the Walsall home and away fan in good times and ill.

Then, over twenty years later, it was Harold Hunter who suggested that scouting might be the niche for me in the game I loved and in which I had up to then participated as minor league and county league player, schoolboy coach and referee. Harold then recommended me to Walsall Football Club as someone who might, in the time-worn phrase, 'do a bit of scouting'.

At that point I owed much to Bill Moore, who appointed me as chief scout soon after taking over as manager of Walsall in 1957. A succession of managers have followed up the early confidence that Bill showed in me by encouraging me and backing my judgment over the years. These include Ray Shaw, Dave Mackay, Arthur Cox and most of all Graham Turner, with whom I was fortunate enough to work at three different clubs.

I have also been very lucky to be supported along the way by football club directors such as Jack Harris, Dick Homden, Ken Wheldon and Tim Yates. Club secretaries, backroom staff, fellow scouts, members of various schools' FAs and players by the hundred from schoolboys to top professionals have become personal friends and have provided me with the host of memories that have made this book possible. Some gentlemen of the press, and especially Paul Marston, have been unstinting in their support over the years.

Forty-seven years is a long time and I am very lucky that I have in general stayed 'match fit' during this time. In this respect I owe so much to Dr A. Kushwaha, Mr A. Cunnington, Mr Ali Khan and 'phone doc' Bill Tweddle from my Wolves days. They were always there when I needed them. Most of all, my wife Molly has been patience personified. Without her I could not have managed it. In recent times she has fielded without complaint a multitude of phone calls from various soccer personalities while Geoff and I have been tucked away writing about them.

Ron Jukes

My heartfelt thanks are expressed to the *Birmingham Evening Mail*, *Derby Evening Telegraph*, *Shropshire Star*, *Express & Star*, Don Stanton and John Bullough for permission to use photographic material. Thanks also to all the soccer personalities for their ready co-operation when I have rung them at all sorts of hours for their memories of Ron. Nor can I ever forget the way Trina and Tracey at Junction 10 have served us with gallons of coffee during the compilation of this book. Nicola, meanwhile, has provided her skilful secretarial services, always with a smile. Last but not least, thanks to James, Holly and all at Tempus Publishing for their patience, guidance and encouragement.

Geoff Allman

# FOREWORD
## by Graham Turner

It is an honour to be invited to write this foreword to Ron's book. Our friendship and professional relationship goes back many years to the time when I persuaded the board at Shrewsbury Town (then enjoying the status of Second Division football for the first time) that the only way forward was to employ the services of a chief scout. It was a luxury for the club and the beginning of my association with Ron that has stood the test of time from Shrewsbury to Hereford via a terrific spell at Wolves.

Ron's like, the all-round scout, are a dying breed, men who may be watching at Stamford Bridge or St James' Park on a Saturday and walking around parks pitches on Sundays hoping for, and occasionally finding, a little gem. His dedication to watching football knew no limits, nor did his keen eye for watching little nuances in a younger player that others had missed. He covered the full range of scouting duties with nothing more enjoyable than, in his own words, 'getting his feet wet' – standing in all weathers spectating. Sometimes he was known to be there, but at other times he would be 'disguised as a tree' when he did not wish his rivals to know he was watching a certain player.

His integrity and persuasive powers are well known throughout the Midlands, often beating off bigger clubs to sign players. Occasionally he has signed the son of a player whom he had signed thirty or so years earlier. He has on such occasions told the lad with unerring accuracy about his dad's ability, where he signed him from and other details. He has often closed the deal by telling the boy what a good player his father was and while the lad was feeling proud of his old man, he would add, 'but he wasn't half as good as you're going to be son.' Dad and lad would be hooked and as good as signed.

Ron's great knowledge of football and strong opinions on the game have earned him tremendous respect across all levels of the game. I have been privileged to know him and to have worked with him through some great times and some difficult ones. His sound common sense and his judgement and advice have always been there when needed, whether people were patting you on the back or stabbing you in it. Ron has been a rock and a pal.

# ONE

# LOOKING BACK

*It's not the hours you put in, its what you put into the hours.*

*Good players, not systems, make good teams.*

As I look back upon almost fifty years of scouting in professional football, various images float before my mind. There was that meeting in 1978 on the car park of a Lichfield hostelry with Walsall chairman Ken Wheldon, manager Dave Mackay and his assistant Des Anderson. Soon we were all inside Ken's Rolls Royce travelling over to Brereton, near Rugeley, where in a rather smaller hostelry a rather nervous young goalkeeper joined us. This was Martin Conneally, whom I had watched playing for a local youth club in the shadow of the cooling towers in that area. Soon he had signed for Walsall and in the next couple of seasons he played regularly for Walsall youth and reserve teams and made three first-team appearances before moving on to Worcester.

Perhaps Martin was not a particularly spectacular signing, but much scouting is unspectacular. Later that evening the foursome of Wheldon, Mackay, Anderson and myself moved a short distance up the road to the Brereton Social Ground. There the home side were playing Alvechurch in the Midland Alliance. In goal for the visitors was a certain Ron Green, whom I had watched some weeks earlier and had been impressed. Dave Mackay became Walsall manager shortly afterwards and encouraged me to sign him, but chairman Ken Wheldon (famous for not spending money if he thought there was the slightest risk) had insisted that Dave, as the new manager, should see the player in action first. Dave had been quite perturbed at Ken's insistence and said 'if Ron is employed as chief scout, then his word should be good enough or what's he here for?'

It did seem to be something of an overkill for four club officials to be watching a young player, but there we all were and, for most of the first half, Alvechurch were so much on top that Green handled the ball only about half a dozen times. Then, close on half-time, Brereton were awarded a penalty after a breakaway. The kick was taken and Ron dived to save confidently. 'That's it, I've seen enough,' said Mackay with some delight. He had backed his chief scout's judgment and made it clear that he regarded the whole episode as superfluous. Off we all went for a drink and next day Green signed for Walsall. He went on to play 265 games for them, plus over 200 more for Shrewsbury, Bristol Rovers, Wimbledon, Scunthorpe and Colchester.

Now another image floats before my mind. I am at Trentham Posthouse Hotel in the Potteries with Shrewsbury manager Graham Turner and I am meeting his chairman, Tim Yates, for the first time. Tim's words are still imprinted on my heart: 'I'm a farmer. I plant my seeds and the Good Lord sends the sunshine and the rain. In the fullness of time, they flourish and bear fruit. I would like you to come to Shrewsbury and plant some seeds for me.'

Next I relive an experience in a dark entry with a barking dog on a winter's night. I had seen Colin Harrison playing for Brownhills Schoolboys in the English Schools' Shield. His all-round ability and attitude made an immediate impression upon me. He had two good feet and was good in the air. In short he could play. I soon discovered where he lived in Pelsall, and so I made my way round to his home that evening. The approach to it, as to many houses in the 1950s and 1960s, was via an entry with the back door on one side and the neighbour's back door on the other side. As I tentatively made my way up the entry, I heard the fierce barking of a dog. I knocked on the door, the barking grew louder and a human voice called out in Black Country dialect the familiar words 'ee wo airt yer'. Thus the first steps towards signing the player who was to make a record 529 appearances for Walsall were taken, through a half-open door to a background of fierce canine barks. He was in fact only a Jack Russell.

The next image is of a typical English day with rain bucketing down. I am in a playing field at Hinckley with four trees adjacent to the pitch and four people beneath them. Under the one tree is Aston Villa chief scout Jimmy Easson. Under the next is Birmingham City chief scout Don Dorman. Under the third tree is Wolves chief scout George Noakes. Under the fourth tree I am getting what protection I can from the elements. All of us are watching the same young player. All of us ended up very wet and, if I remember correctly, the player we were watching went to Southport.

Then there were the first steps towards signing future Welsh international Carl Robinson for Wolves. This young midfielder hailed from Abergavenny in mid-Wales and he had impressed me in a seven-a-side tournament in Anglesey. We invited him to Molineux to look around and a little later I invited his parents, a delightful couple, to come to a first-team game as our guests and suggested that they park by the West Park. Imagine my disappointment when, a few days later, I rang to enquire whether they had enjoyed the day out and learned that they had picked up a parking ticket. I asked them to send it to me so that Wolves could pay it. Some time later, and before Carl actually joined Wolves, I found myself in the Walsgrave Hospital in Coventry for bypass heart surgery. The Robinsons were the first of many to send me a get-well card. Scouting has many sides to it.

# TWO

# RON JUKES THE PLAYER

*Don't play fancy football in your own penalty area.*

*Play the ball the way you're facing. You can never see what is behind you.*

It is not a prerequisite of the successful scout to have been a brilliant player himself. I certainly was not a brilliant player, though opinions vary as to exactly how good or bad I was. I was, however, a well-intentioned one who always enjoyed the game and always gave 100 per cent to it. Like most lads born in the late 1920s, I enjoyed kicking a ball around in my spare time. I was brought up in the Caldmore Green area of Walsall, opposite the Forum Cinema. I was the eldest of three children, my sisters Barbara and Pat both being younger than me. My dad owned a grocery business (noted for its boiled ham) and I attended Whitehall Infant and Junior Schools. There, under the guidance of sports teacher Phil Jowett, I played numerous practice games for the school team, though when the actual game came round I always seemed to be reserve. I participated in all the sports that I could and became a particularly strong swimmer.

In 1939 I passed the entrance examination to Queen Mary's Grammar School, Walsall, but my starting date was delayed while air raid shelters were constructed, war having been declared on 3 September. I have vivid memories of lessons being interrupted and going down those shelters when the sirens sounded. I also remember rotas being drawn up for fire-watching, with a group of senior boys sleeping in the dining room and a member of staff sleeping in the staff room.

Queen Mary's was a rugby playing school and in the upper school I did well as a place kicker, often roared on by the stentorian voice of Miss E.M. Flint (later to become mayor of Walsall and founder of the Hydesville School). Although I enjoyed rugby, especially the place kicking, my heart was not really in the oval ball game. One of my contemporaries was Phil Giles, who would subsequently play seventy games for Walsall in the Third Division (South) in the late 1940s and early 1950s. Phil and I were frowned upon by the school sports masters for preferring to play football for Walsall YMCA rather than represent the school at rugby. Phil and I played football and cricket together for many years. He was a fine all-rounder.

I did play for the school at cricket under the captaincy of Malcolm White, who was later to keep wicket for Cambridge University and occasionally for Warwickshire, and Stan Davies. After the Second World War I continued to play football and cricket and I must have impressed someone as, in 1946, I was signed by Wolves' chief scout George Noakes. For a time I fluctuated between Wolves' various junior sides and at one time played in a half-back line alongside Bryn Smallwood and Eddie Russell. Eddie went on to make over 150 Football League appearances for Wolves, Middlesbrough, Leicester and Notts County in the 1940s and 1950s.

My time with Wolves was relatively short, but I continued to play in the Walsall Minor League. In the YMCA team that I captained, I played alongside future Walsall players Peter Atkinson, Joey Boyden and Jack Bridgett and against future Aston Villa goalkeeper Graham Cordell, George Dean and Ron Russon in the highly successful Hillary Street Old Boys' team. Ray Russell, a future Shrewsbury Town and Crewe forward, was also among my opponents in those days, playing for Bloxwich Youth Club.

I was also pleased to be selected for the Staffordshire youth side, which consisted of players from the North Staffs Minor League and the Walsall Minor League in roughly equal proportions. My teammates there included future Port Vale and Portsmouth defender Basil Hayward and Ronnie Allen, who went on to score over 300 League and cup goals, most of them for West Brom, and to play 5 times for England. I met up again with Ronnie in 1973 when he managed Walsall for a short spell while I was chief scout there. At that stage I had ambitions of going to university, but although I enjoyed going to Oxford to take a scholarship, I was unsuccessful. Then, when I was accepted conditionally by one university, I failed to meet the requirements in Latin. I therefore proceeded to Saltley Teacher Training College. There I played a number of games for the college side captained by Harold Hassall, who went on to play for Huddersfield and Bolton and to win five England caps.

I shall never forget the opening remarks of the college vice-principal, Mr Jim Chance. In his first lecture to new entrants to the college, his first words were: 'Gentlemen, practice does not make perfect… (long pause) …only PURPOSEFUL practice.' He went on to say, 'Gentlemen, have a good opinion of yourselves… but make sure that it is realistic.' These words were the basis of his lecture and they have stayed with me until this day.

After a few weeks at Saltley, I received the college principal's permission to go home at weekends because of my mother's illness. This enabled me to play football for a number of sides including Walsall Wood, where one of my teammates was Derek Pace, who was destined to score over 200 Football League goals for Aston Villa and Sheffield United. I also had a few games for Walsall's 'A' team in the Birmingham League in 1947/48. Gilbert Alsop, who had scored the opening goal in Walsall's memorable FA Cup win over Arsenal in 1933, was then in charge of the Walsall team, leading the attack himself while Billy Bennett was in goal and Charlie Humphries and Ray Clutton were in defence. I vividly recall a game at Worcester when I received a painful blow in the nether regions from Worcester player-manager Jack Vinall, who had played for Walsall in the previous season. I can still feel it! I also recall thefts during a game at Gloucester when the dressing rooms were ransacked.

After a brief start to my teaching career at Great Wyrley Secondary School (near Walsall) where T.P. Riley was headmaster, I was called up for national service in the RAF in 1948. I did my square bashing at Padgate and was then posted to take an equipment course at Hereford. There my ability to write on a blackboard was utilised by a Sergeant Wright, who relished getting some of his work done by a sort of unofficial 'teacher's assistant'. Soon after Christmas I was posted to Stafford 16 M.U., where I took on the role of equipment assistant on number 6 site. While I was there, a new pilot officer arrived and was given the responsibility of cataloguing the library in the officers' mess. He passed on the job to me and I was given two hours per day free of other duties to enable me to do this. This meant a long walk to the library each day, but I didn't mind this break from the normal routine.

In those early days in the RAF I played in inter-wing games but then, after breaking an ankle while playing for Walsall YMCA one weekend, I was not only out of the game for a time but was nearly arrested as a deserter, as I had failed to return to my unit on account of the broken ankle. Fortunately the station medical officer who came out to Walsall with two Redcaps to arrest me recognised me as the airman who had been cataloguing the officers' mess library, where he was an avid reader, and I was allowed an extra few weeks to recover.

After returning to Stafford upon my recovery I worked in the maintenance unit for the rest of my national service with two hours per day in the officers' mess library as I had done before my injury. I was also fortunate enough to receive a 'living out' pass. So much for my national service! During the football season I was thus able to play for several local sides and during the cricket season I played for Walsall second and third teams in the Birmingham League on Saturdays and for Blakenall on Sundays. For Walsall my teammates included Jack Dutton, George Lowbridge, Freddy Stokes and Eric Wait, while at Blakenall I played alongside men such as Phil Canning, Graham Cordell (later to play League football for Aston Villa and Rochdale), Ray Law, Rod Bell and Don Peacock. I continued to play for Blakenall for over twenty years, most of them as captain.

Upon demobilisation I worked successively at North Walsall Secondary School, Bluecoat Junior School, North Walsall Secondary School (this time as head of English), Butts Junior School and then in a scale post at North Walsall Junior School. In each of these posts I spent as much time as possible developing the football, cricket and swimming in the school. I also became team manager of Walsall Schoolboys Under-15s, a responsibility that came to an end in the late 1950s after I had become a scout for Walsall FC. Someone found a regulation that stated that the person in charge of the schoolboys' team could not be connected with a professional club. That someone then secured the post for himself.

After Walsall Minor League secretary Harry Giles had suggested that I take a referees' course, I refereed for a time in the Walsall Minor League, but this did not bring me the satisfaction that playing football or working with schoolboys in football, cricket and swimming had done. Most school days, after teaching, I stayed well into the evening with eager young players. I still cherish memories of those days and I still meet and talk with some of my protégés from those days. I enjoyed these after-school sessions as much as the boys and I am happy to have raised the standard of sport in the schools. It can in fact be said that the playground cricket at Bluecoat School produced an England fast bowler in David Brown.

# THREE

# SCOUTING – HOW IT BEGAN

*A scout who cannot make his mind up is of little use to anybody. What is a real scout?*

*You don't win any medals for bravery on the halfway line.*

The late 1950s were momentous times in my life with joys and sorrows intermingled. In 1957 I lost my father after a six-month battle against cancer. My mother was in hospital with a long-term illness. Consequently a major event in my life was put back to 1958 when I married Mary Capeling at St Matthew's church, Walsall. I had met Mary (or Molly as she was known) while we were both on the staff of Bluecoat Junior School. She had arrived in Walsall straight from college in Derby, but was a native of the North-East and a Sunderland supporter, her particular hero being Len Shackleton.

A few months before my marriage my scouting career had also taken off when I linked up with Walsall Football Club, the team I had followed for over twenty years. My first link with the club had been in the 1930s when Ivy Beavan, a teenage family friend, who was a sort of unofficial childminder to me to prevent me getting underfoot in my father's shop, took me to Fellows Park to see the pre-war Saddlers, who played at that time in claret and blue. Though I was only six or seven years old, I vividly remember players such as teenager Bert Williams (the future England goalkeeper), defenders Jack Shelton, Norman Male and

Lew Morgan, midfielders Bill Bradford and Bill Simpson, wingers Reuben Woolhouse and Charlie Bulger, former Northern Ireland international striker Joe Bambrick and the one and only Gilbert Alsop. Gilbert had scored the opening goal in Walsall's legendary FA Cup win over Arsenal in 1933 and, after spells with West Brom and Ipswich, had returned to Walsall in 1938/39 and at one stage netted 16 goals in the course of 5 games. Johnny Hancocks and Wally Brown were then in the reserves. Ivy also introduced me to cricket at Walsall's Gorway ground and I saw such players as former England man 'Tich' Freeman, Norman Backhouse, Norman Partridge, Vic Tromans and a little later Dick Howorth, Jim McConnon and Danny Mayer. I acted as scorer for the first team for a time during the Second World War and then played in the second immediately afterwards.

As far as football was concerned, I continued to watch Walsall during and after the Second World War when I wasn't playing myself and, as mentioned in the previous chapter, played a few times in their third team in 1947/48. My links with local football had up to this time included playing, coaching and refereeing. Then one day Harold Hunter, chairman of the YMCA for whom I had played and who was also on the Staffordshire FA and a lifelong Walsall supporter, suggested that I try my hand at scouting. Harold was at that time a commentator for the Walsall Hospitals Service and he had a conversation with Mr H.W. Bonner who was on the Walsall Hospital Board and was a Walsall FC director. As a result I was invited to watch players in games first at Atherstone and then at Oswestry.

In both cases the players I had been sent to watch did not impress me as likely to make the grade in League football. The Atherstone goalkeeper was a good shot-stopper, but was on the small side and tended to save at the expense of corners. The Oswestry midfielder who had been recommended to Mr Bonner (who had links with the Oswestry board) did not impress me as anything more than a useful player at that level. Walsall officials were expecting positive reports on these two players, but my judgments and the reasons for them were accepted. Incidentally, I still use the criterion of whether a goalkeeper concedes corners by reason of his height. I often wonder what would have happened if I had recommended the two players in question.

At that time Walsall were managed by Jack Love, a former Nottingham Forest inside forward who had been player manager for a time after succeeding Major Frank Buckley as Walsall boss in September 1955. By Christmas 1957, however, he had been succeeded by Bill Moore. Bill had been a no-nonsense defender with Stoke and Mansfield before the Second World War and in more recent times had been trainer first of Notts County and then of Aston Villa. Many of the Villa FA Cup-winning team of 1957 attributed their success to Bill, who had the reputation of being a hard man with a strong emphasis on physical fitness. He had been brought to Walsall by Ernie Thomas, another hard man who had made a success of his canal barge business and had given Bill carte blanche to appoint his own staff.

Bill was, in general, not impressed with the players that he found at Walsall when he arrived. Having appointed Vic Potts, the former Aston Villa defender, as trainer he expressed his intention of bringing in new players. To help him in his quest his eyes fell on me. I was one of the few scouts connected with Walsall at that time. Apart from any football knowledge I may have had, Bill seemed impressed by the fact that I was a trained teacher and presumably had a standard of literacy that would enable me to help him with his correspondence and newspaper articles. This I did. Accordingly, with very little scouting experience behind me, I was appointed chief scout to one of football's hard men and was given the task of setting up a modus operandi for scouting at Walsall. From that moment on I found myself out at matches most nights of the week. I shall always be grateful for the opportunity Bill gave me, taking a gamble on my ability to do the job, which I came to love.

Bill was keen to strengthen the Walsall front line in particular, so as to provide support for Tony Richards, a striker who had been signed in 1954 after being released by Birmingham and writing in for a trial at Walsall. He had scored 68 goals in three-and-a-half seasons in a struggling side. Other assets among the players that Bill inherited included former West Brom defenders Harry Haddington and Eric Perkins, former Bury and Stalybridge central defender Albert McPherson and powerful midfielder Tim Rawlings, who had been a junior with West Brom.

In those days scouting was less well organised than it is today. It was generally assumed that ex-players would make good scouts. Clubs were informed of promising young players from a variety of sources. Many of those recommendations would end up in the wastepaper basket but if there seemed good reason to follow up a tip, managers would put their scouting (such as it was) into operation. In fact, Midlands clubs such as Aston Villa, Birmingham and Wolves were among the most intense searchers after talent and it was Bill Moore's intention that Walsall should follow their example.

In my early days as Walsall's chief scout I accompanied Bill to several local grounds and quickly got to know scouts of other clubs, such as Nobby Clarke and Paddy Ryan at West Bromwich, Don Dorman at Birmingham and George Noakes at Wolves, who incidentally had signed me as a junior some years before. I also met up with football reporters, such as Charles Harrold of the *Birmingham Gazette*, an excellent local morning newspaper now sadly long out of existence.

Soon after Bill Moore had appointed me, he had put me in touch with a Mr Mason, who had a fruit and vegetable business at Wordsley near Stourbridge. He was an Aston Villa fanatic and had had many an after-match drink with Bill during his Villa days. He had contacted Bill about a striker who was making an impact with Stourbridge and who worked in the Birmingham meat market. Accordingly, I rang Mr Mason and soon I was travelling with him to see this young striker in action in a game at Hereford. Quite honestly I was not at all impressed, but I did say I'd have a second look at the boy. In fact I was using him as a decoy, as my real interest was in a flame-haired winger on the Stourbridge side. He was strong on his left side, had ability on the ball, directness and an eye for goal. Even on a muddy pitch he had shown outstanding ability. I explained to Bill what I had seen and he realised just how impressed I was, and arranged for Walsall vice-chairman Neville Longmore to accompany me to have a second look at the young winger, so that he could handle any financial issues that may arise. Stourbridge were playing Nuneaton the next week and, to cut a long story short, a deal was struck in the boardroom at half-time. The winger in question was Colin Taylor and Neville also signed his inside forward partner Peter Jeavons, the combined fee being £500 if I remember correctly. Peter did not make the first team at Walsall and returned to Stourbridge at the end of the season, but Colin went on to score 190 goals in three spells with Walsall.

On the following Monday evening Bill and I went over to Stourbridge to get the signatures of Colin and Peter. Peter was in a cinema and his name was flashed on the screen to ask him to meet us outside. Colin was in a record shop and we linked up with him there. Mr Mason was somewhat perplexed that we did not sign the striker he had recommended and expressed doubts as to whether Colin would make the grade, but he continued to send us the occasional recommendation over the years. I always tried to look at these as I respected his judgment and I was grateful to him for his part in the Colin Taylor signing. What's more, Stourbridge had fielded some good players over the years and before the Second World War had sold future England man Pat Beasley to Arsenal.

My time as Walsall chief scout had thus begun well as, within two months of my appointment, I had landed a player who was to become one of the club's greatest ever goal-scorers. Another important move as far as I was concerned occurred shortly afterwards when I heard that Bill Moore had moved out of his club house in Walsall. I asked the chairman Ernie Thomas whether I could purchase it and he kindly agreed, letting me have it for the price the club had paid for it several years before. I am still living in it over forty years later.

Results did not immediately improve at Walsall. In the second half of 1957/58 they ended the season in twentieth spot in the old Third Division (South). It was at this time that there was a dramatic reorganisation of the lower divisions with the Third Division (North) and Third Division (South) being replaced by the Third and Fourth Divisions, with the top twelve teams in each section of the old Third Division forming the new Third Division and the other teams forming the Fourth Division. Walsall thus found themselves in the new Fourth Division and Bill set about building a promotion team. Before the end of 1957/58 he had signed both goalkeeper John Savage and striker Roy Faulkner from Manchester City. These moves came about through pre-war Wolves and Brentford defender George Poyser, with whom Bill had worked at Notts County. George then lived in Sale, near Manchester, and one Friday evening Bill and I went to a game at Stockport and called on George on the way there for a cup of tea and to exchange information.

Then, in the summer of 1958, I responded to Bill's request to 'find me a winger who is brave' by recommending Colin Askey, who had played over 200 games for Port Vale, including an FA Cup semi-final against West Brom in 1954, and was still only twenty-six. Colin went straight into the Walsall team at the beginning of 1958/59 as did Peter Woodward, a goalkeeper whom I had seen on several occasions for West Brom reserves. Peter was, however, only standing in for big John Savage, who was starting the season under suspension. Another useful player signed at that time was midfielder Arnold Walker from Grimsby. Arnold made only occasional first-team appearances but always did well. He was also a useful cricketer and played for Blakenall, the team that I captained, both as a batsman and a medium-paced bowler. I felt that he could have held his own in Minor Counties cricket.

Though Walsall never quite looked promotion material in that first season in the Fourth Division, they did manage to finish sixth at a time when play-offs were still nearly thirty years into the future. It was interesting to see Kenny Hill making his first-team debut towards the end of that 1958/59 season. He was twenty at the time and had been signed from Bescot United before my appointment as chief scout, but he had been one of my pupils at North Walsall Boys' School. I had seen him progress to the Walsall boys' team as a member of a strong half-back line alongside Roy Peach and Roy Shepherd. Both Roys also had spells on Walsall's books, though neither broke through into the first team. Kenny Hill actually made his League debut as a defender, but it was in midfield that he went on to play over 100 games for Walsall in three different divisions. He shares with Brian Caswell the distinction of being one of the two players whom I taught in school and later saw develop into Football League players.

Before the end of 1958/59 I had recommended the signing of Scunthorpe winger John Davies, this being another instance of going to see one player and being more impressed by another. I had actually gone to watch a Southport player (they were of course still in the Football League at that time) but it was visiting Scunthorpe winger John Davies who took my eye. Playing wide on the right, he was fast and, in addition to having a good right foot, was a fearless header of the ball when crosses came in from the opposite flank. I felt flattered when Bill announced the signing of John in the local newspaper with the words 'strongly recommended by the chief scout'.

The close season of 1959 was an active one. John Sharples, who had been on amateur forms with Walsall as an inside forward a few years earlier, was signed after being released by Aston Villa where Bill Moore had known him during his time there. By this time he had developed into a tall full-back and had been strongly recommended by former Villa defender John Neal. I had seen him on many occasions in Villa reserves and agreed. Then there was goalkeeper John Christie, who had been in the Southampton side beaten by Walsall in an FA Cup tie in December 1955. John had mishandled a cross on that occasion, but he became a key figure in the Walsall sides of 1959-1961, able to talk to his defenders and with a powerful left foot with which to effect clearances. He was a steady, reliable, influential goalkeeper.

Another interesting signing during the summer of 1959 was Trevor Foster. He was one of the few players I remember signing after he had written in for a trial. He was a pupil at Joseph Leckie School, who were not affiliated to the Walsall Schools FA, and so their pupils were not eligible for selection by Walsall Boys. Leckie had an outstanding team at that time, however, and when invited alongside several other Leckie boys to play in a trial game at Pleck Park, Trevor immediately impressed with his ball control and ability to glide along on his long legs in a manner not dissimilar to that of Steve McManaman in a later era. I signed Trevor in the treatment room at Fellows Park after the game. Then, the following October, Frank Gregg graduated from the ground staff to the professional ranks, the first player to do this in Bill Moore's time. He was a most reliable young defender who hailed from Kinver Street, Wordsley, near Stourbridge. I vividly remember visits to his home while he was still at school. Bill Moore took him under his wing and helped him to develop into one of Walsall's best ever defenders. As Frank's career developed so did the fortunes of Walsall FC and he served them well in two promotion seasons, two seasons in the Second Division and then several seasons back in the old Third Division, playing in a total of 444 first-team games.

Knocking on doors such as the one in Kinver Street was the normal practice for scouts and chief scouts in those days. One could then approach schoolboys but not sign them until they left school or until (after a change in the rule) their fourteenth birthday. The knocking-on-the-door approach gave the opportunity to build a relationship with the young player's family. On the other hand, co-operation from junior clubs varied considerably. Some would favour particular League clubs so that it was difficult for a scout from another club to make progress towards signing a player.

Within two years of my appointment as Walsall chief scout the club seemed to be running away with the Fourth Division in what was the second season of its existence. Seven successive games were won in October and November 1959, with 26 goals scored in the process. It is often, however, a good time to sign players when a team is enjoying a successful run and in December 1959 another important piece was added to the promotion jigsaw with the signing of Jimmy Dudley from West Brom. Two young players, Stan Jones and Peter Billingham, had just moved to The Hawthorns and Jimmy, after over 300 games for Albion, was finding it difficult to hold down a regular first-team place. He had been in the Albion FA Cup-winning team of 1954 and he was still a quality player. I had seen him on numerous occasions in both Albion's first and reserve teams and I liked him. His elder brother George had guested for Walsall during the war years and I was delighted to get the signature of Jimmy, who could play on either the left or right of midfield. At thirty-one, I felt that he still had some good football left in him and, happily, I was right as he went on to give Walsall over four years' excellent service. Jimmy was an immediate success in the second half of that 1959/60 season as Walsall romped to promotion with a total of 102 goals. What a transformation Bill Moore had brought about in a side that was in the lower reaches of the Third Division (South) when he took over two-and-a-half years earlier. No fewer than five players scored more than 10 goals, with long-serving Tony Richards (24) and Ken Hodgkisson (11) joined on the scoresheet by three players who had come to Fellows Park during my time as chief scout, as Colin Taylor got 21, Roy Faulkner 22 and John Davies 12.

As one looked at the prospect of life in the new Third Division in the summer of 1960 it seemed that quality players such as Roy Faulkner and ex-West Brom men Ken Hodgkisson and Jimmy Dudley would again be able to deliver the goods and that, while that prolific front line from 1959/60 would continue to score goals, a defence playing in front of

John Christie might well be able to cope with most Third Division forwards. There was no talk of first-team pools in those days, but Bill Moore was keen to have cover in vital positions and to that end defender Granville Palin was signed from Wolves. He was able to play on either flank or in the centre, possessing two good feet and being a good header of the ball. He had been a member of the Wolves youth team that had turned round a 5-1 first-leg deficit in the 1958 FA Youth Cup final to win 6-5 on aggregate against a Chelsea side that included Jimmy Greaves. Granville was also a useful cricketer who had played for Coseley Crusaders, a wandering side for whom I had frequently guested. He also played alongside me for Blakenall and went on to play for Walsall seconds in the Birmingham League. I had used the time when I played cricket with him to help persuade him to sign for Walsall Football Club. A football scout is never off duty.

Defensive strength was also enhanced by the signing of Tony Eden, whom Bill Moore had known as a reserve central defender at Villa Park and who has in recent years made his mark as groundsman there. Walsall got off to a good start in the Third Division with 7 wins and 2 draws in the first 12 games. During this spell they actually scored one more goal than they had done in the first twelve games in the Fourth Division the previous season. Bill Moore was, however, still looking for more forward strength and I was sent to watch former Middlesbrough striker Arthur Fitzimmons, who had won 26 Republic of Ireland caps while at Ayresome Park. He was then at Mansfield and it was while watching him in action there that I overheard in the boardroom that Mansfield were hoping to sign Tommy Wilson, who had scored for Nottingham Forest in the 1959 FA Cup final but was no longer a first-team regular. This signing, however, depended on them selling Fitzimmons to Walsall. I let Bill Moore know of this while he was in the bath at Fellows Park the following Monday morning and after a quick discussion Bill contacted Eric Houghton (his manager when he was at Villa Park) who was then working in the Nottingham area. Soon Tommy was a Walsall player – a real opportunist signing. Both Bill and I were delighted.

Tommy was an immediate success, holding the ball up well and scoring 9 goals in that 1960/61 season. He was also a major factor in Tony Richards increasing his goal tally from 24 in the Fourth Division to 36 in the Third Division. Colin Taylor also increased his goal tally from 12 in the Fourth Division to 33 in the Third Division and Walsall gained promotion for the second season in succession, ending the season with 10 wins and a draw in the last 12 games. During the season Colin Askey had come back from injury to take over from John Davies on the right flank of the attack, and John left to join the police force in Portsmouth. Colin actually scored the goal that clinched promotion at Shrewsbury on a memorable evening in April 1961 with a flying header – that had been John's particular strength. A record Shrewsbury gate of 18,917 saw this game, more than half of them from Walsall.

Meanwhile, young players continued to be recruited as one looked to the future as well as the present. This was given a higher priority at Walsall at this time than ever before. Young goalkeeper Alan Boswell, a fanatical trainer who regularly stayed at the ground in an evening long after the other players had gone home, was signed in 1960. I also signed young forwards Colin Jukes and Arthur Hodgetts from the West Bromwich area. Neither played in the first team, but they strengthened the youth side and it made it easier to sign other young players if they were joining a successful team, as Walsall were now becoming.

As we contemplated the forthcoming 1961/62 season in the Second Division after two successive promotions we signed diminutive winger George Meek, who had had a spell on loan to Walsall from Leeds during Major Buckley's time as manager. George had just had a season with Leicester in the old First Division, and was a real bag of tricks playing wide on the right. Bill Younger also moved from Nottingham Forest in readiness for the new season and, though he wasn't with Walsall for long, he did score a fine match-winner into the Hillary Street goal in the second home game of the season against Newcastle in front of a record Fellows Park gate of 25,453.

With seven members of the team that had come up from the Fourth Division two seasons earlier, Walsall managed a respectable fourteenth position in the Second Division and, had it not been for a serious shoulder injury suffered by Tommy Wilson after scoring both goals against Luton on Boxing Day, the position could well have been higher. One of the revelations that season was teenager Alan Boswell (mentioned above) who took over in goal from John Christie in November and held his place for the rest of the season. His dedication to training had certainly paid off and at this stage some saw in him a future Bert Williams. There were few additions during the 1962 close season. Maurice Partridge, a determined but unpolished defender from Birmingham City, had the bad luck to make his debut in an early season 6-0 home defeat by Newcastle, while Mick Pearson, a former Midland schoolboy, came from Manchester City and played just three games up front. Meanwhile Gordon Wills, an FA Cup finalist in his Leicester days, was a skilful inside forward but not fully mobile after a ligament injury, though he was later to play some useful games in midfield and captained Walsall for a spell.

One mid-season signing was striker Jimmy O'Neill, whom Bill Moore brought down from Sunderland just before Christmas. Bill had disappeared for two days and no-one at the club knew where he was, but he had in fact gone to visit friends in the North-East who had told him about Jimmy. Things looked promising when Jimmy netted twice on his debut against Portsmouth but not only did Walsall lose the game 5-3, but because of the severe winter there was an amazing seventy-seven-day gap before the next game could be played. No-one will ever know how much that long lay-off contributed to Walsall's relegation at the end of the season, but relegated they were after losing the final game 2-1 at home to Charlton with only nine fit men in those pre-substitute days. A point would have kept them up, but goalkeeper Alan Boswell was taken to hospital after a collision and Graham Newton was a limping passenger for much of the game.

So after those heady days of promotion in successive seasons Walsall were now back in the Third Division and the situation was not helped when Alan Boswell was transferred to Shrewsbury after a verbal clash with unforgiving chairman Ernie Thomas. Shrewsbury had just suffered a worse tragedy when goalkeeper Paul Miller died in a swimming accident. I had signed Paul for Walsall a few years earlier and, because there were several young goalkeepers at the Saddlers at the time, he had moved to Shrewsbury in 1959 and had played over 100 games for them. I was pleased to see Boswell, one of my best ever discoveries, fixed up quickly with first-team football again but disappointed at the reason he left Walsall. I reflected sadly on the tragedy of twenty-two-year-old Miller and remembered visiting his home at Haughton near Stafford when signing him.

With Colin Taylor moving to Newcastle in the close season and Tony Richards and Tim Rawlings going to Port Vale, it was something of a new-look Walsall that kicked-off back in the Third Division in August 1963. Former Wolves junior Malcolm White had been signed from Grimsby to take over in goal and it was rather ironic that so soon after having a surfeit of goalkeepers Walsall now had to go out and sign one. Jimmy Fell, a winger from Lincoln City with his best days probably behind him, was also brought in, as was Graham Matthews, a striker with a powerful shot who had impressed in a League Cup game against Walsall and whom I had seen in Central League games for Stoke on a number of occasions. Then there was Ron Howells, a midfielder from Scunthorpe who had begun his career with Wolves. He played a few good games, notably when continuing to play at the heart of the defence in a 2-1 win at Peterborough after having a broken ankle strapped up. Little did anyone know then that a few weeks later he would be in court, answering charges of taking bribes in his Scunthorpe days.

Early results were not good and Bill Moore resigned in December after six seasons, in which unprecedented success for Walsall had been followed by an unhappy season and a half. Reserve-team trainer Alf Wood, the former long-serving Coventry goalkeeper, took over and I was left to think back over Bill's time at the club. He had given me my chance as chief scout. He had come to the club at a time in their history when they could hopefully only move one way. He had proved to be the man for the job. He was nearer to the team than most managers are. He was widely respected after his FA Cup success at Aston Villa. He was acquainted with many Midland hostelries. He had many ex-player contacts and friendships. He was a real Geordie character. In reality it was sad for me to see him go. Little did I know then that he would be back for a second spell at Walsall just over five years later.

In the meantime Walsall struggled, before narrowly avoiding a second successive relegation at the end of 1963/64. I could, however, feel a certain amount of satisfaction that several young players whom I had brought to the club had shown promise in League football. David Tennant, a local schoolboy from Carless Street, less than a mile from the ground, had done well in goal, saving a penalty in his first away game at Brentford. Speedy Roger Smith, a schoolboy from Tamworth, had attracted Wolves' attention with his displays on the right wing and was unlucky to suffer an injury just as Wolves were about to sign him. Ray Wiggin had come from Rushall Olympic after a spell with Aston Villa and had impressed with his heading ability up front. He had scored a fine goal in the 5-1 defeat at Bristol City. Alan Roper from Tipton had looked a much better player after moving from midfield to defence. Most exciting of all, Stan Bennett, the former captain of Aston Schoolboys, had won the hearts of fans with his powerful displays at the heart of the defence and occasionally in midfield. Allan Clarke, another ex-ground staff boy and one of the five brothers from Short Heath who played League football, had looked a class player in the few games he had played up front, while in the last game of the season Nick Atthey, a North-Easterner by birth whom I had spotted in Coventry schoolboy football, made his debut at QPR. Allan was destined to move on to Leeds and England stardom after nearly three seasons with Walsall, while Stan and Nick stayed on to become two of the greatest club servants ever to play for Walsall – a real manager's joy.

And so to 1964/65 and the emergence of a further bunch of young players in the reserve side who were playing in the West Midland League. These included Brian Horton, Roy Cross and Bobby Gough, who all went on to play in League football and clocked up over 1,000 games between them, and David Brookes, a powerful defender who spent a number of seasons in Midlands non-League football. The first team, however, got off to a poor start with a home defeat by Gillingham and a 5-1 hammering at Bristol City when defender Frank Kletzenbauer, whom Alf Wood had bought from Coventry late in the previous season, broke a leg and was not fit for first-team action again. Two close-season signings, defender John Leedham from Millwall and midfielder Graham Chadwick from Manchester City, failed to impress and in October first manager Alf Wood and then chairman Ernie Thomas left the club. Oddly enough, although only 3 of the first 18 games had been won, one of these was by a 4-0 margin over QPR and another by a 4-1 margin over Reading, with Allan Clarke getting a hat-trick in the latter game.

I was sorry to see Ernie Thomas go. He had been the chairman throughout my time as chief scout. A rough diamond, Ernie had grown up working on barges and literally fighting for the right to go through locks first, but he had seen Walsall twice win promotion. He had always called a spade a spade and had shown complete confidence in Bill Moore and myself to produce a winning team. He had said on one occasion, 'If Bill wants to field the groundsman then that's all right by me.' He was succeeded as chairman by industrialist Bill Harrison, a 'friend' and sparring partner who had resigned from the Walsall board a few years earlier after a disagreement with Ernie. Soon Bill was bringing in his own men as fellow board members, among them former referee Bill Clements, former Birmingham City secretary Walter Adams and local men Reg Hargreaves and Ron Sillett, while Eric Wood, who had been on the board some years earlier, returned. He also brought in former Birmingham midfielder Ray Shaw, initially as physiotherapist and then as manager. Ray was a native of Walsall and, some years earlier, on his way to catch the bus to training at St Andrews, had seen me playing in a kick-around game on some waste ground near Delves Common. When we linked up at Walsall in 1964 as manager and chief scout respectively he told me how, without knowing who I was, he had been impressed by the way I seemed to be 'bossing' the game intelligently and organis-ing the whole group of lads. 'There's a lad who knows the game,' he had said to himself. I hoped that he still felt the same later after we had worked together.

How lucky I was that the new manager was someone with whom I could establish a close working relationship, just as had been the case with Bill Moore. Yet Bill and Ray were vastly different personalities; Bill the blunt North-Easterner, Ray the quiet Black Country family man. Bill was constantly out and about while Ray, though always ready to go on a scouting mission when he felt it necessary, liked nothing better than to be at his home fireside. Both, however, respected their players and were respected by them, and both were excellent communicators.

I was delighted with Ray's early moves in the transfer market as he sought to turn round Walsall's 1964/65 season. Colin Taylor, my first signing for Walsall way back in 1958, was brought back from Newcastle. Good solid professionals were brought in from the Midlands area that Ray and I knew so well. These included defenders John Harris and Graham Sissons, John from Wolves and Graham, a former Birmingham man, from Peterborough. Ken Satchwell, a former Coventry winger, was brought in from Nuneaton and former Aston Villa ball player Jimmy McMorran was brought back to the Midlands from Third Lanark in Scotland. Bill Harrison was, however, keen to make a really spectacular signing and one Thursday asked me where I was going on the following Sunday. I told him I should be watching Sunday games on the local Redhouse Park. This was just a stone's throw from Bill's house in Fairyfield Avenue, Great Barr, and Bill asked me to call in for a cup of tea after the park games had ended. In the course of conversation on the Sunday he asked me what I thought of signing either defender Trevor Smith from Birmingham or skilful ball player Peter Broadbent from Wolves. I wondered at the time how far he had discussed these players with Ray Shaw, but I ventured the opinion that I had long been a great Broadbent fan. I was therefore disappointed when, a few days later, Walsall signed Trevor Smith. As it turned out Trevor had to retire through injury after only 12 games for Walsall, while Broadbent went on to give five years' good service to Shrewsbury, Aston Villa and Stockport. Yet, though the signing of Trevor Smith did not work out, most of the other signings did and the fact that the young Stan Bennett was, at twenty-one, turning in some excellent performances at the heart of the defence, meant that Trevor's contribution was not really missed. The blend of up-and-coming players and seasoned professionals helped Walsall climb from nineteenth place in 1964/65 to ninth in 1965/66.

The blending of youth and experience had served Walsall extremely well in the 1959-1961 promotion seasons and Ray Shaw was just as strong an advocate of this policy as Bill Moore had been. A perfect example of this blend was provided by the striking partnership of George Kirby and Allan Clarke. George, a devout Roman Catholic, had seen service with Everton, Plymouth, Southampton, Coventry and Swansea before landing at Fellows Park in the summer of 1965. He was thirty-one at the time but it seemed that there was plenty of good football left in this powerful striker with the delicate touch who could provide some steel when the going got tough. He was just the sort of experienced professional that nineteen-year-old Allan Clarke needed to play alongside. In just seven months together they totalled 38 goals between them with Clarke getting 15 before moving to Fulham (from where he went on to Leicester and Leeds and played 19 games for England). Allan was a wonderful one-on-one player in a similar category to Jimmy Greaves. George went on later into management and I watched a few games for him when he was in charge at Halifax and I was between jobs.

Apart from the vast improvement in their league position, Walsall also figured in two memorable cup ties in that 1965/66 season. A crowd of 41,118 were at The Hawthorns to see them go down rather unluckily 3-1 at West Brom, with Nick Atthey having a goal disallowed when the score was 1-1. Then, in the FA Cup, they pulled off a tremendous 2-0 win at First Division Stoke with ten men for over half the game, after Jimmy McMorran had been injured by a crunching tackle in what was the last season before substitutes were allowed in FA Cup ties. The opening goal at Stoke had been scored by experienced winger Howard Riley, who had moved from Leicester a few weeks earlier. Howard was a fine crosser of the ball with an explosive shot on occasion, and was an example of Ray Shaw and I looking out for and being prepared to wait for the sort of player we needed, rather than signing a useful-looking player just because he had become available.

Even after Allan Clarke had moved to Fulham in March 1966 goals continued to flow as the man signed to replace him, Harry Middleton, got 14 goals in 18 games before the end of the season, including four in one game against Gillingham on Easter Saturday. Harry was a former Wolves junior who, after just one first-team game for the Molineux men, had moved successively to Scunthorpe, Portsmouth, Shrewsbury and Mansfield, and had usually looked good when playing against Walsall. Harry's great strength was that he knew how to score goals. Harry was still only twenty-nine when he came to Walsall, while another player to attract attention in 1965/66 was only just over half that age. This was Geoff Morris, a former West Bromwich schoolboy who, at the tender age of sixteen, had made a successful first-team debut against Peterborough. When I had first seen him at the age of fourteen I thought he would become one of the finest players I had ever signed. I saw him as the man ultimately to succeed Colin Taylor at Walsall and then go on to a top team, but he was held back by suffering from asthma. Even so, he still had a useful Football League career with 45 goals in 267 games, 41 of the goals for Walsall before moving on to Shrewsbury and Port Vale.

With the blend of youth and experience available, Walsall fans looked forward to the 1966/67 season with confidence. In football, however, just one incident can seriously affect prospects. In the opening game of the season, against Mansfield, skipper John Harris suffered a serious knee injury and was never fully fit again. That opening game was lost and, although the team gave some good performances from time to time, the final position was no higher than twelfth. Fortunately, twenty-year-old Mick Evans came through from the reserve team to take over on the left side of the defence, but John's inspirational leadership was missed. I had signed Mick from Vono Sports in 1964 and, after 263 games for Walsall, he went on to have useful spells with Swansea and Crewe and was still scouting for me at Telford nearly forty years later.

Another success story of that 1966/67 season was Allan Baker who, in his first season at Walsall, not only excelled as a ball player but also got 16 goals. The one he scored in a League Cup tie at Exeter when he went past man after man is still talked of by those who saw it. I was particularly happy to see Allan doing well. I had played alongside his father Dennis some years before when I was guesting for Toll End Wesley while at Wolves. Dennis in midfield and Jack Bache in defence were the stars there. Allan had first come to prominence with Brierley Hill Schoolboys, where he formed an impressive right-wing partnership with Norman Ashe. Both played for England Schoolboys and both signed for Aston Villa. A broken collarbone had prevented Allan from winning a regular first-team place at Villa Park but he was now fully fit again and, at twenty-two, he seemed to be an ideal signing for Walsall. He was skilful and thoughtful with excellent close control and was a regular goal scorer. After four good seasons with Walsall, however, Alan's career was ended by a serious knee injury in September 1970. Once again, a good signing had been made from what might be termed the 'Midland Patch'. One of the positive sides of signing players from the local area was that one knew what one was getting. My regular visits to Central League games not only in the West Midlands but a little further afield in the East Midlands and the Potteries paid off time and time again as I was able to form a clear idea of a player's consistency as well as his ability.

Another feature of that 1966/67 season was Walsall's use of three different first-team goalkeepers. Terry Carling had come from Lincoln in exchange for Malcolm White in 1964 and had missed only one game in the next two seasons. Early in 1966/67, however, the less consistent Bob Wesson had been signed from Coventry, where Walsall coach Arthur Cox had known him some years earlier. Bob was on the wrong end of a 6-2 hammering at Oldham in only his fourth game for Walsall and, although he went on to play some good games, Bob did concede the occasional goal that fans felt could have been prevented – and they let him know their feelings on the subject.

Towards the end of that 1966/67 season Bob was replaced by Keith Ball, who was then in his second spell at Walsall after returning from Worcester. Keith was popular with fans, having first joined Walsall from Wolverhampton Road Schools and having played a few good games in the old Second Division. One couldn't help reflecting, however, that most successful teams over the years had fielded a regular goalkeeper and few have fielded three or more in a season.

At this particular time I felt that there was some intrusion from above into the scouting process. Chairman Bill Harrison had 'friends' on other West Midlands clubs' boards, and he was instrumental in signing former West Brom and Birmingham midfielder Alec Jackson in February 1967. Though he scored some useful goals (notably the match-winner in the FA Cup replay at Crystal Palace in January 1968 to earn a fourth round tie against Liverpool) Alec lacked that vital ingredient of consistency.

In the meantime there were a number of promising local players who were unable to win regular places in the Walsall first team, among them Trevor Meath, whom I had signed from Darlaston for £500 after he had done well in a game against Walsall in what was then the West Midlands League. Roy Cross, a former Walsall Boys player, clocked up just a handful of first-team games for Walsall and Port Vale before injury ended his career. Then there was Bobby Gough, who had been in the Erdington team that had won the English Schools' Shield but who was released after just one first-team game for Walsall. He went on to score over 100 league goals for Port Vale, Southport and Colchester, with a happy combination of skill on the ball and an eye for goal.

Brian Horton has, in more recent years, become something of a household name as both player and manger, but he did not play even one first-team game for Walsall after I had spotted him as a youngster playing for Cannock Schoolboys. I had in Charlie Wright a great ally in the Cannock area when he was scouting for me. I labelled him 'the best drinker of bad tea in the country', such was his ability to watch young footballers in all sorts of unlikely and likely places. Charlie's son David was a promising goalkeeper who had a short spell as a Walsall reserve and later played for Chasetown. His career, however, did not bear comparison with that of Brian Horton, who went on to play over 600 games for Port Vale, Brighton, Luton and Hull and to become an outstanding captain. He has since held several managerial appointments and is in charge at Macclesfield at the time of writing. Nor must we forget Graham Allner, a highly promising winger signed by me for Walsall from Alvechurch. He scored twice in one reserve game against Northampton in the Football Combination at a time when Northampton fielded their first team but, like Brian Horton, never played in the Walsall first team. He went on to become well-known in management with Kidderminster, AP Leamington and Cheltenham. This tendency not always to recognise the talent of young players landing at Fellows Park was by no means rare over the years.

Reference has already been made to Bobby Gough in the late 1960s and in the 1970s Roger Davies was released after a trial, and went on to play regularly in Derby County's 1974/75 First Division Championship side. In the 1980s Stan Collymore was released after playing for Walsall at youth-team level and way back in the 1940s Derek Pace, whom I had played alongside at Walsall Wood, had a trial game with Walsall but was not taken on. Though slightly built as a striker, Derek went on to score over 200 goals for Aston Villa and Sheffield United. He later worked as a traveller for Walsall chairman Bill Harrison's Triplex Company, and was actually signed for Walsall in 1966, just eighteen years after that original trial game. It was too late for Derek to be really effective but he did score one memorable flying header in a game at Grimsby in August 1966.

Another veteran signed in 1966 was former Aston Villa winger Jimmy Macewan. At one stage in 1966/67 he alternated between playing on the right wing for the first team and acting as reserve-team trainer. He was a grand clubman and a typical Scot. I well remember going with him on a scouting mission to Stirling. We stayed overnight at Carlisle on the way there and at the game met Walsall club doctor Ron McKechnie, who was a native of those parts. We intended to stay again at Carlisle on the way back but Jimmy, having purchased a haggis from a shop he knew, decided we could get back home soon after midnight, and this we did.

There were still hopes in the summer of 1967 that promotion might be on Walsall's agenda despite the disappointing final position of twelfth the previous season. New signings included Jimmy Murray from Manchester City. Jimmy had been a member of Wolves' 1958 and 1959 League Championship sides. Meanwhile Arthur Cox moved to Villa Park as Tommy Docherty's assistant. Arthur had made a great impact at Walsall after joining them as their youngest ever coach in 1964.

Close-season signings included defender Jack Burckitt from Coventry and midfielder Mick Tindall from Aston Villa. Jack didn't make the first team and Mick played only 8 games. Hopes that one or more of the young players at the club (these included midfielder Terry Mighalls from Rugeley and strikers Gary Fleet from Friar Park Wednesbury and Frank Carsley from Erdington) might come through did not materialise, Frank having the bad luck to suffer a broken leg. Despite a Stan Jones match-winner in the opening game at Shrewsbury, results were disappointing. The team's finest display was probably in the third round FA Cup tie against Spurs in January when Dave Wilson, the new striker from Grimsby, had a shot cleared off the line by Joe Kinnear before Jimmy Greaves got a late winner for Spurs.

Shortly afterwards manager Ron Lewin was sacked, and fans were thrilled to hear in February 1969 that Bill Moore had been reappointed as manager, just over five years after leaving the club. In between times he had been scouting for Fulham, had suffered a broken marriage and his son had emigrated to Australia. I looked forward to young players being given an opportunity by Bill, as had happened during his previous spell in charge, and fans wondered whether he could take Walsall back to the Second Division again. Lightning rarely strikes in the same place twice, however, and few managers achieve significant success in a second spell with a club. Even so, some outstanding young players appeared for Walsall during Bill's three-and-a-half seasons back with the club.

Colin Harrison was the one survivor on the playing staff from Bill's previous time at Fellows Park and he continued to fulfil his early promise in a variety of positions. Ray Train, whom I had signed from Bedworth, had some useful games in midfield before moving on to Carlisle and a variety of other clubs, while two of the finest goalkeepers ever to play for Walsall had spells in the first team before moving on. I had signed

Phil Parkes a couple of years earlier from Brierley Hill Schoolboys during Ray Shaw's time as manager, but he was actually released at one stage. I blew my top at what I saw as criminal maladministration and rushed to his house, where I found the massive figure of Phil draped over two chairs watching television. Soon he was back at Walsall again. In April 1970 Bill Moore gave him his first-team chance and Phil took it with both hands, playing 60 successive games before moving to QPR at the end of 1969/70 and going on to play well over 700 League and cup games. But for his career overlapping those of Peter Shilton and Ray Clemence he would surely have played many more than a solitary game for England. Just over a year after Phil's move to QPR another tall goalkeeper was signed by Walsall. Mark Wallington from Sleaford, Lincolnshire, was recommended to Eric Houghton, who was then a Walsall director. Mark was about to sign for Lincoln, but we invited him for a trial game and I signed him immediately. Within days he was making his first-team debut as a non-contract player in a 2-2 draw at Torquay in September 1971. He went on to play just 12 first-team games. Probably his finest game was the FA Cup tie at Everton in February 1972 when 45,462 saw him keep Walsall in the game as they went down 2-1. Shortly afterwards he moved to Leicester, where Ray Shaw was chief scout, and succeeded Peter Shilton in the Foxes' goal. At one stage he played in 331 consecutive games for Leicester and later joined me again at Derby.

Bill's second spell with Walsall was also a good time for strikers. Six months after Bill's return, we managed to sign Colin Taylor for a third spell, on this occasion from Crystal Palace, to whom Dick Graham had sold him during his short spell in charge sixteen months earlier. In addition Bill was delighted when two young strikers found their way to Fellows Park – with a bit of help from me. Early in 1971/72 a well-built striker named Bernie Wright wrote in for a trial. I fitted him up in a trial game at Darlaston along with other young talent. His power in the air and on the ground created an immediate impression and I suggested at the end of the game that he play for Walsall reserves the following Saturday. Bernie was not convinced that I had the authority to make this offer and insisted on speaking to manager Bill Moore. Bernie was a big man who towered over me and so there and then I rang Bill from the treatment room at Fellows Park. Bernie was reassured when Bill confirmed my offer of a game in the reserves. Soon he was in the first team and scoring on his debut against Port Vale. A few weeks later he played in the FA Cup tie at Everton in which Mark Wallington so impressed, and shortly afterwards Everton signed him on the strength of his performance in that game. He had played just 20 games for Walsall by the time of this move, but after trouble behind the scenes at Goodison Park he returned a year later to Walsall and starred in the FA Cup wins over Manchester United and Newcastle in January 1975. I vividly remember travelling to Castle Vale near Birmingham in search of Bernie when I heard that Everton were prepared to release him. It was a foggy night and I was about to take a torch and look for numbers on doors when a well-built figure came down the road. I approached this figure for guidance and discovered to my delight that it was Bernie himself.

During Bernie's brief spell at Everton I managed to sign another striker who was to make his mark in League football. Bobby Shinton, a West Bromwich boy, was playing for Lye Town at Kidderminster when I saw him and at half-time I spoke to Lye chairman Charlie Floyd about the possibility of signing Bobby for Walsall. Charlie readily agreed and Walsall paid a small fee and also gave Lye the old Fellows Park floodlights. At the same time I tried to sign another striker, Keith Leonard from Highgate. In fact, both Keith and Bobby played in a trial game several days later at Fellows Park. This was behind closed doors and consisted basically of the Walsall first team against the reserves. Both Keith and Bobby got hat-tricks. After the game both were taken to the boardroom. Bobby signed immediately but Keith, who was accompanied by the Highgate manager Nobby Clarke, hesitated. He expressed a wish to have a trial with Aston Villa before making up his mind. In fact, he signed for Villa a few days later. Sadly, after scoring 11 goals for Villa and having a loan spell with Port Vale, Keith's career was ended by injury. Bobby meanwhile scored on his debut for Walsall against Swansea and got two more against Bradford City a week later. Bobby, who was a glazier by trade, spent two years with Walsall and went on to play for Wrexham, Cambridge, Manchester City, Millwall and Newcastle and later had a spell as player-manager of Worcester.

It was during this spell of successful signings that I got into trouble for an alleged illegal approach for the only time in my career. I was looking for players for the Walsall youth side in 1971 when I saw a winger named

Jimmy Dainty playing for Northfield. I approached the Northfield team manager for permission to approach Jimmy and this was readily given. In due course Jimmy was signed. Technically I should have made the approach through the Northfield secretary, a Mr Hill. The Birmingham FA upheld this rule and I was fined £5. In due course I signed Jimmy at his house in Coleshill on a Sunday after another seven days' notice had been given. He played several times for the Walsall youth side and made 5 first-team appearances before moving to Ireland.

Another player signed in that 1971/72 season made a total of 247 first-team appearances. This was versatile Brian Taylor from Coventry who, at various times, played well in defence, midfield and attack. He also played cricket for Blakenall, whom I was captaining at that time, and later played League football for Plymouth and Preston before his untimely death at the age of forty-six.

Throughout Bill Moore's second spell as manager a steady flow of young players was coming through. Among them was Alan Birch, a midfielder from Stone Cross, West Bromwich. He not only played in the youth team at sixteen but, like Geoff Morris eight years earlier, made his first-team debut at sixteen and went on to play 191 games in midfield before moving on to Chesterfield, Wolves, Rotherham, Scunthorpe and Stockport. Joe Mayo, a young striker from the Dudley area, played only 2 full first-team games (oddly enough in defence) before being sold to West Brom for a small fee and then going on to Leyton Orient, Cambridge and Blackpool. He now runs a hotel in North Wales.

For the 1972/73 season John Saunders had been signed from Leeds, midfielder Willie Penman from Swindon and striker John Woodward from Aston Villa, and the team won 9 of their first 13 games and fans wondered whether Bill Moore was going to lead the club into the Second Division, just as he had done twelve years earlier.

Although it is true to say that managers are rarely successful in two separate spells with a club, Bill Moore saw his side survive a relegation scare in 1970/71 and then enjoy a run of 17 successive League games without defeat at the end of 1971/72 and the beginning of 1972/73. In fact, a promotion run was looking very much on when Walsall won 9 and drew 1 of their first 13 games of 1972/73. What's more, the team at that time contained seven home-grown players: Frank Gregg, Mick Evans,

Colin Harrison, Stan Jones (in his second spell), Nick Atthey, Bobby Shinton and Geoff Morris. Then came disaster in the midst of an unhappy game at Brentford on 14 October 1972. There was a bitter disagreement between Bill and the coach John Smith over the substitution of defender John Saunders for the striker Chris Jones in the midst of a 2-0 defeat. Bill resigned the following weekend, though it was not clear whether there had been other issues at stake besides that substitution. So for the second time in nine years I found myself regretting the departure of the man who had first appointed me as chief scout in 1957. I had worked well with him during both his spells with the club and I shall always respect his encouragement of good straightforward football and his readiness to give young players every chance to make good.

John Smith, who had come to Walsall as player-coach in the summer of 1971, was appointed to succeed Bill. He was a skilful ball player who had seen service with West Ham, Spurs, Coventry, Leyton Orient, Torquay and Swindon and had been capped by England at Under-23 level. He had played just 13 games after joining Walsall, having at thirty-two lost some of the mobility of his heyday. Only 1 of John's first 8 games in charge was won and any promotion hopes petered out, but he did make one interesting move in the transfer market in January 1973 when he exchanged skilful little winger Geoff Morris for experienced striker George Andrews from Shrewsbury. George was thirty-one when he joined Walsall, but he stayed long enough to score 38 goals in 177 games in four-and-a-half seasons and will always be remembered for his headed match-winner against Newcastle in the fourth round FA Cup tie in January 1975 on a muddy Fellows Park. George did not have the best of debuts for Walsall, figuring in a 6-2 defeat at Grimsby in January 1973. This proved to be the last of Bob Wesson's 220 games in goal for Walsall, though he later played for Burton Albion. Bob was one of seven goalkeepers used by Walsall in 1972/73. Reference has already been made to local lad Keith Ball and the others were Glen Johnson, on loan from Aldershot; John Osborn, on loan from West Bromwich Albion five years after figuring in their FA Cup-winning side; Ian Turner, on loan from Southampton; Dennis Peacock, on loan from Nottingham Forest; and Jimmy Inger, a non-contract player from the Nottingham area who had been recommended to chairman Ken Wheldon while he was playing for Long Eaton United.

John Smith's unsuccessful five months in charge ended with his resignation in March 1973. Only four games were won during this period but
I felt that John Smith was doing his best, always being ready to watch
games. He made a particular point of watching youth football on Sundays.
Sometimes he and I watched schoolboy football together, and I well
remember his honesty when he said that he was lacking in confidence
when watching schoolboys. On one occasion he said to me 'Tell me
who can play. I can't judge lads at so young an age.' I wish other so-called
'experts' were as honest.

After John Smith's resignation in March 1973, Jimmy MacEwan
ended the season as caretaker manager with the team ending up in
seventeenth place – a sad disappointment after their good start. Yet
there were at least two bright spots before the end of the season. In a
remarkable Tuesday evening game in March, Walsall came back from
a 3-2 deficit to score twice in injury time to beat Bristol Rovers 4-3.
Lion-hearted Stan Bennett had performed heroically in that game after
sustaining a broken nose and one of the two late goals was laid on by
sixteen-year-old Alan Birch, who was making his debut as substitute in
a game that seemed to go on and on as the referee played over a quarter
of an hour's injury time. Then, in April 1973, Walsall battled to a 3-2
win over Chesterfield, with Brian Caswell making his debut just two
months after his seventeenth birthday. As mentioned elsewhere, Brian
shared with Ken Hill the distinction (if that is the word for it) of being
taught by me in school and then playing for the Football League team
of which I was chief scout. Brian was a splendidly versatile player who
made a total of 483 appearances for Walsall before moving to Doncaster
and then Leeds, where injury virtually ended his playing career, though
he did play a solitary game for Wolves in 1987.

By the beginning of the following season (1973/74), former England
and West Bromwich Albion striker Ronnie Allen had taken over as Walsall
manager. I had played in the same team as him for the Staffordshire
Under-18s in the 1940s and he had a tremendous record as a player, with
a total of 354 goals for Port Vale, West Bromwich Albion, Crystal Palace
and England. Ronnie was unfortunately less successful as a manager, not
being the best motivator of moderate players. Some useful signings were
however made during that 1973 close season. Goalkeeper Mick Kearns

came from Oxford having already been capped by the Republic of Ireland. He did not miss a game for over three seasons, won another 15 Republic of Ireland caps and totalled 332 games for Walsall. In 2006 he is still working for the club as goalkeeping coach and Community Liaison Officer. Roger Fry came from Southampton and made his debut on the same day as Mick on the opening day of the 1973/74 season. He went on to play 136 games on the left side of the defence and provided the perfectly placed free-kick from which George Andrews headed the winner in the famous FA Cup win over Newcastle in January 1975. Roger's consistency meant that Frank Corrigan, a young player with a strong left foot, whom I had signed after seeing him play for Blackpool, chalked up only one first-team game for Walsall. After a spell with Burton Albion he returned to League football with Wigan, played over 100 games for them and became their regular penalty taker.

With John Saunders on the right side of the defence and Roger Fry on the left there were precious few chances for Keith Brown, who came through from the junior ranks to make his first-team debut in a 2-0 win at Blackburn in December 1973. In another era he would surely have made more than the 10 first-team appearances that he made in 1973-1975.

Dwarfing all the other signings made during Ronnie Allen's time in charge, however, was that of Alan Buckley, the diminutive fair-haired striker who came from Nottingham Forest, scored a League Cup hat-trick against Shrewsbury on his home debut in August 1973 and went on to score 205 goals in 483 games in his two spells with Walsall. During my second spell at Walsall I worked closely with him when he was manager and since then we have continued to consult each other on the merits of various players. His name, like those of previous Walsall strikers Gilbert Alsop and Tony Richards, was synonymous with goals.

Ronnie Allen resigned just before Christmas of that 1973/74 season and, after a spell in which the club claimed to be run by a players' co-operative, Doug Fraser emerged as the next manager. He had had a fine playing career with West Bromwich Albion and had won two Scottish caps. He joined Walsall as a player in the summer of 1973 after two-and-a-half seasons with Nottingham Forest. He was, however, often beaten for pace at this stage of his career and he did not increase his popularity with fans by being sent off in a game against Bristol Rovers in November 1973 after a skirmish with former West Brom colleague Kenny Stephens, who had himself been with Walsall in the late 1960s. Doug was himself turning out in the reserve team early in 1974 and, after a crushing 8-0 defeat at Bristol City, he complained to the Walsall board that there were no players with future prospects coming through the youth ranks. Accordingly, I was summoned to a board meeting and it was suggested that I needed some experienced help. I was offered the services of a certain Tony Senter to work alongside me. I just did not fancy being dictated to in an area in which I had had sole responsibility for sixteen years and I resigned rather than attempt to link up with the gentleman suggested by the chairman and secretary. Tony Senter had previously scouted for short spells for Brighton and Derby and I believe that his main claim to fame was that while at Derby he had recommended striker Roger Davies from Worcester City. I couldn't help remembering that I had seen Roger playing in a Wolverhampton Amateur League representative side some years earlier and had taken him for trial games at Walsall. The management at that time, however, decided not to take him on and Wolves also turned him down soon afterwards. He had then moved to Worcester via Bridgnorth. Before I left that board meeting, secretary John Westmancoat suggested that the club needed to have a scout in every county in the land and I pointed out to him, tongue in cheek, that in counties such as Devon and Cornwall the only discoveries would be cows or sheep. I could not see that such a suggestion would bring in more effective players. Despite the views of those gentlemen, it is a fact that geographical location is a vital factor in recruiting talent and many young players prefer to join a club within striking distance of their homes. As it turned out, Tony Senter was with Walsall for only a comparatively short time and not one of his discoveries ever made the first team. Meanwhile, of that reserve team that Doug Fraser had spoken so disparagingly about, Alan Birch and Brian Caswell steadily developed into regular first-team players, Kelvin Clarke had a few games in the first team before suffering a serious injury and John Jones got a hatful of goals at reserve-team level. What's more Gary Shelton, who was on the ground staff when I left, went on to play 645 League and cup games in a career of over twenty years. He is, at the time of writing, reserve-team coach at West Bromwich Albion.

I was very unhappy to leave Walsall at this point. The criticism seemed so unfair. I knew probably better than anyone the youth talent that was already there and I was continually looking for promising young players. One young player I left behind was Mick Tuohy, a West Bromwich-born striker and a staunch Catholic. He was in the youth team when I left and without me to press his claims he did not break through into the first team. After a spell with Redditch he went on to play 20 games for Southend in 1979/80 and played in non-League football up to the age of forty.

FOUR

# TO BIRMINGHAM – AND THEN BACK TO WALSALL

*Try to play most of the game in your opponents' half.*

*A good call is as good as a good pass.*

I was not long away from the scouting scene after leaving Walsall early in 1974. One of the first approaches came from Wolves, with their manager of that time Bill McGarry offering me a job that would require me to report directly to him quite independently of the scouting system that was then in place at Molineux. I was uneasy about this. I was also approached by the long-serving Birmingham City chief scout, Don Dorman. Don had been a dynamic inside forward with Birmingham, Coventry and Walsall in the 1940s and 1950s after recovering from injuries sustained in the Arnhem landings in the Second World War. Both offers had their attractions and I turned to former Walsall manager Ray Shaw, himself an ex-Birmingham player, who was by this time chief scout at Leicester City. I had of course worked with Ray during his time in charge at Walsall and my friendship with him had continued. He recommended that I take the Birmingham offer and this I did. Soon I found myself at St Andrews linking up with Harry Birch, a good, honest local scout who had served the club for years. Don's instructions to Harry and I were for us to keep a close eye on talent in the West Midlands while Don himself covered the West Country and London.

Life was very different at St Andrews from what it had been at Fellows Park. I was instructed to watch specific games at places such as Chester, Chesterfield, Derby, Sheffield and Runcorn. In many cases I was covering what for me was new territory as Birmingham's net for schoolboy talent was cast far wider than Walsall's. Large *pro formas* were provided on which detailed reports were to be made and handed in. Two players on whom I recall doing favourable reports but who were not signed by the Blues were future Arsenal and England striker Paul Mariner and Peter Withe, who was then in Wolves' reserves and who did in fact join the Blues after I had left. He too went on to play for England and scored the match-winner for Aston Villa in the 1982 European Cup final.

One player whom I watched who did sign for the Blues was winger Steve Fox, a Tamworth schoolboy. Scouting was very much a team affair at St Andrews and another scout I worked alongside was former Blues midfielder Malcolm Beard. Don Dorman would, from time to time, meet his fifteen to twenty scouts over a weekend to discuss how things were going. When I joined the Blues, former Manchester United midfielder Freddy Goodwin was manager, but early in 1975 he moved to America and was succeeded by former Leeds midfielder Willie Bell. John Aston Senior, the former Manchester United defender, also joined the club around this time as 'adviser' and, in my latter time there, I found myself sending in reports to him rather than to the chief scout, Don Dorman. It was a club for which I had respect, but I was not so involved as I had been at Walsall and as I was to be at other clubs, and I did not enjoy the job so much. I didn't really feel that I was doing myself or the job justice.

While I was at Birmingham I continued to follow events at Walsall with interest. Dave Mackay succeeded Doug Fraser as manager in March 1977. At the same time I was invited by chairman Ken Wheldon to return to the club I had left just three years earlier. I chatted with Alan Hill, the former Rotherham goalkeeper and long-standing friend and fellow scout. Alan, who knew Dave well, said that he was an excellent man to work for though he laughingly told me to avoid accompanying Dave on any scouting trips to Scotland as these tended to last several days.

Dave had brought Des Anderson, a one-time Millwall and Hibernian midfielder, as assistant manager and, after accepting the job, I felt that I was very lucky to be working with two such men in attempting a rescue

act at Walsall, the team I had grown up with. I was, in fact, now returning to the post of chief scout to which I had first been appointed nearly
twenty years earlier.

Dave soon made his presence felt. Not only did he take over the secretary's office and bring in a leather settee and a mini bar but, more
significantly, he turned results round to such an extent that the Walsall
team that was in danger of relegation at the time of his appointment lost
only 2 of their last 15 games and ended the 1976/77 season in fifteenth
place in the Third Division. It was very gratifying for me to see two
of my signings from my previous spell at Walsall, Alan Birch and Brian
Caswell, in the first team and in fact Alan got a hat-trick in the 5-3 win
at Peterborough in the last away game of the season.

The momentum was maintained in 1977/78 as Dave used his East
Midlands contacts to bring in players such as Henry Newton, Tony Macken,
Jeff King and Graham Moseley from Derby County. Henry was unfortunately afflicted with muscular problems by this time and dropped out in
mid-season. He later scouted for me when I was at Derby County. Tony
went on to play over 200 games for Walsall, most of them on the right side
of the defence, and Jeff King was a powerful midfielder whom Mackay and
Anderson really liked and who had two useful seasons at Walsall. Graham
Moseley, meanwhile, was taken on loan to fill the temporary gap in goal
when Mick Kearns was out for the first time in three seasons.

Ron Green, whose signing from Alvechurch was described in the early
part of this book, also made his debut in goal early in Dave Mackay's reign
and Gary Shelton and Ian Paul kept up the steady flow of young players
into the first team. Gary, to whom reference has already been made with
regard to the 600-plus League and cup games that he ultimately played
for a variety of clubs, was a Nottingham schoolboy who had been playing for a team managed by my long-standing friend and fellow Blakenall
cricketer Graham Cordell. I had first known Graham when he was playing
in the Walsall Minor League in the 1940s. He went on to play League
football for both Aston Villa and Rochdale and for many seasons opened
the innings with me for Blakenall Cricket Club. Graham then moved to
the Nottingham area and created and managed a team called Parkside
who were the close rivals of Clifton All Whites, the junior team that Ken
Wheldon had unsuccessfully adopted as a Walsall feeder team during Tony

Senter's time as chief scout at Walsall. Sadly, Graham died at the early age of fifty-six, by which time Gary Shelton was in the midst of a highly successful Football League career. He made his Walsall debut as a skilful inside forward at the age of eighteen and less than two years later was sold to Aston Villa, ultimately playing for no fewer than eight different League clubs over a period of twenty years. His last club was Chester, for whom his son Andy also played.

Another young player at Walsall in the late 1970s was Ian Paul. Ian came from the Wednesfield area, attending the same school as Paul Jones, the midfielder who joined Walsall some five years later. Ian's father was the Aston Villa kit man and when he and his wife announced that they were moving to Chester Road, Erdington, so that they could take on the responsibility for Aston Villa's young professionals at the club hostel, I hurried to sign Ian for Walsall. He made his debut at the age of seventeen and quickly established himself in the first team. He was equally happy in defence and midfield and, but for a serious medical condition that ended his League career in December 1980 after 83 first-team games and 11 goals, he would, in my opinion (an opinion that Dave Mackay shared), have gone far in the game. Offers for him were already coming in from top clubs at the time when his illness struck just before his twentieth birthday. This illness was a tragedy for himself, his family and for Walsall Football Club.

Making his debut on the same day in April 1978 in a game at Preston was Don Penn, a teenage striker. I had first seen Don play in the Campbell Orr Shield in a Handsworth League representative side at Cadburys, Bournville. I had immediately been impressed by his pace and powerful shooting and I contacted the Newton Albion manager Harry Maney, the team for whom Don played, and signed him. Don became a key figure in Walsall's 1979/80 Fourth Division promotion side with 26 goals, but sadly his career was ended by injury when he was just twenty-two. This was another tragedy for Walsall and for this lion-hearted little striker, who was very popular with fans.

A final position of sixth in the Third Division in 1977/8 would have earned Walsall a play-off place if play-offs had been in existence in those days. It did earn Dave Mackay and his team a celebratory party at chairman Ken Wheldon's large house in Whittington, near Lichfield. Sadly, however, Dave moved to Kuwait in the summer of 1978 to manage the

Arabic Sporting Club. Dave always had his eye to business and I benefited on one occasion from his successful tie company. Hearing that it was my birthday he took me to his car, opened the boot and offered me the pick of a multitude of ties.

How much Dave was immediately missed by Walsall was indicated by the fact that they lost the first three games of 1978/79. Alan Buckley had started the season as a caretaker manager while continuing to play, but was then succeeded by Alan Ashman, a prolific goalscorer for Carlisle in his playing days who had later managed the Cumbrians and taken them to the old First Division for one season in 1974/75. I well remember being requested to travel on the team coach for Alan's first away game in charge of Walsall. This was at Chester and I was even invited to his pre-match team talk. I was quite amazed by what I heard. Alan exhorted everyone to be 'on your toes', dancing backwards and forwards to add emphasis to his words. It was something akin to a scene from a farce, but the result was no laughing matter as Walsall lost 2-1 with Jimmy Kelly, the former Wolves winger, scoring on his debut.

Alan brought in experienced players such as Steve Waddington from Stoke City. Steve, a midfielder, was the son of Stoke manager Tony Waddington, with whom Alan had a close friendship. Another addition to the Walsall staff at this time was former Birmingham defender Ricky Sbragia, who in more recent times has been reserve-team manager at Sunderland and among the backroom staff at Manchester United. Results, however, were disappointing and by the second half of the season it was clear that Walsall were fighting a relegation battle. Dave Syrett was signed from Swindon to try to boost the goal tally but, apart from two goals in a late-season 2-2 draw at promotion-seeking Swansea, things did not go well for Dave. I had hopes that Jimmy Williams, a Wolverhampton-born player who had been scoring regularly for Worcester City and for whom Walsall paid a small fee, might make an impact up front, but he had the misfortune of coming into a team that had got used to losing. He played in the last 11 games of the season, none of which were won, though he did manage to score 3 goals.

Though Terry Austin, a striker signed from Plymouth late in Dave Mackay's reign, had scored 13 goals by March, he was transferred at this point to Mansfield. By now Frank Sibley, who had served QPR both as player and manager, had succeeded Alan Ashman as Walsall's manager, but there was no halting the slide as Walsall slipped down to the Fourth Division in May 1979. Despite his lack of success at Walsall, Frank was a very likeable character and, despite having a seriously ill son in London that meant him travelling up and down the M1 daily, he never missed a training session. He also had the ability to go out for a meal and eat virtually every dish on the menu, as I well remember from a visit to a game at Shrewsbury and a visit to Bromsgrove when we were signing striker Steve Round. He was also an intrepid driver and I well recall travelling with him on icy roads to an FA Cup tie at Shrewsbury one Friday evening. He had not one bit of luck during his brief time at Walsall, but I do wonder whether relegation might have been avoided if Eddie Clamp had been signed from Stoke when he became available earlier in the season, as it was the sort of battling qualities that Eddie possessed that were missing in the vital last weeks of the season when only 5 points were picked up from 10 games.

Another major factor in the slide to relegation in 1978/79 had been the transfer of sharp-shooter Alan Buckley to Birmingham early in the season. Alan's goals were sadly missed, as was his infectious enthusiasm. Even so, I was not too pessimistic about the future as young players Ron Green in goal, Kenny Mower in defence, Paul Jones in midfield and Don Penn, Mark Rees and Paul Waddington up front had all made occasional appearances in the first team. The problem was that in 1978/79 there were not enough quality experienced players to keep results ticking over while young players were introduced. This is important for any club, that results keep coming while the future is being prepared for.

The summer of 1979, however, brought a major coup when striker Alan Buckley was re-signed from Birmingham City for the same fee that the Blues had paid for him nine months earlier. This was an attractive proposition for chairman Ken Wheldon, who appointed Alan as player-manager and saw it as getting two jobs done for the price of one. Alan saw it as the first step up the ladder of management and it seemed that everyone was happy when there was an immediate upturn in both results and morale. Though Walsall went out of the League Cup in the first round to Chester, they were unbeaten in the first 13 League games of 1979/80. Buckley himself got 7 goals during this spell and went on to get 18 in the season.

The promotion momentum was maintained, with only 5 games lost all season, though Walsall were edged out of top place by Huddersfield in the final reckoning. Young players Ian Paul, Kenny Mower, Brian Caswell and Don Penn all became first-team regulars in this promotion season, with Don getting 26 goals in his first full campaign. I wondered what former manager Doug Fraser, who was by this time working in the prison service in Nottingham, thought of all this. It was he who had announced just five years before this that Walsall had no young players coming through. What perception!

Roy McDonough, who had come from Birmingham in the previous season, provided experience up front and Dave Serella, in his sixth season, was a key figure in defence so that the blend of youth and experience seemed to be coming good once again. Another young player who made his debut near the end of that promotion season was defender John Horne, a Dudley boy who had come on a YTS from Brierley Hill Schools. John was a typical Black Country lad, as rugged a defender as one could meet and though he played in only sixteen Football League games he went on to play in Midland non-League football for over twenty years. What a competitor!

As one looked forward to life back in the Third Division I was pleased to sign Richard O'Kelly from Alvechurch in the summer of 1980. I had to be patient when the kick-off of a pre-season Alvechurch *v.* Newport game was delayed because the visitors were held up by holiday traffic on the M5. The game was well worth waiting for as Richard, who was playing up front for Alvechurch, impressed me immensely. He showed that he had two good feet, held the ball up well, particularly with his back to goal, and was a good finisher, getting a hat-trick in a comfortable win for Alvechurch. He went straight into the first team in August 1980, as did two experienced players, Peter Hart from Huddersfield and Steve Baines from Bradford City. Peter came as a midfielder but did much better when he dropped back to a sweeping role and became captain. He is nowadays proving to be just as good an influence as a Church of England vicar, and recently moved to a church in Cannock. Steve, after two seasons as a rugged defender, moved to Scunthorpe and is now a Football League referee.

Walsall struggled to avoid relegation from the Third Division in both 1980/81 and 1981/82, but two of my signings played a major role in the dramatic last-minute escape in May 1981. Playing at Sheffield United and needing a win to stay up and send United into the Fourth Division for the first time, Don Penn netted a late penalty to put Walsall in the lead and then Ron Green saved an even later penalty to preserve that lead. A few weeks earlier busy little David Preece, a publican's son from Bridgnorth, had made his debut. I had first seen him playing for Bridgnorth Colts and I had some difficulty in fixing him up with digs when he first came to Walsall. He was one of the busiest little players I had ever seen and had a delightful left foot. He was to be a key figure in the Walsall side that reached the Milk Cup semi-final of 1984 and was later in the Luton side that beat Arsenal in the League Cup final of 1988. I met up with him again in 2003/04 when he became first-team coach at Telford.

Two of my last signings in my second spell at Walsall were Lee Sinnott and Craig Shakespeare. When Lee made his first-team debut in March 1982 he followed in the footsteps of Geoff Morris and Alan Birch, who had been signed by me for Walsall and had made their first-team debuts at the age of sixteen. He went on to become a highly efficient defender with Watford, Bradford City (three spells), Crystal Palace, Huddersfield and Oldham. While Lee was still only eighteen when he moved from Walsall to Watford, Craig stayed long enough to play 355 games in midfield before moving to Sheffield Wednesday in 1989. He had a tremendous left foot that brought him 60 goals with the most powerful shooting we had seen from a Walsall player since the days of Colin Taylor. Craig is at the time of writing a coach at West Bromwich Albion, and we frequently chat on the telephone.

Sadly, however, by 1981 things were not good behind the scenes for a chief scout at Walsall. After being asked by manager Neil Martin (who had taken over from Alan Buckley for a spell) to watch Huddersfield Town, who we were due to play in an FA Cup tie, permission was withdrawn by the chairman. Restrictions were put on phone calls and the last straw came when I was forbidden to sign non-contract players without the permission of the chairman. In the past several of my best signings had been made when I moved quickly to sign young players before other clubs snapped them up. I felt that the directives that were now coming from the chairman and secretary made my position as chief scout quite untenable. I resigned after a late-night board meeting following a midweek game in March 1981. Soon after I arrived home a Walsall director rang me just after midnight asking me to reconsider, but there was no turning back. I was leaving behind a number of good friends, including Alan Buckley and Neil Martin, who had shared managerial duties during the previous two seasons. Alan had encouraged young players to play good football when they came into the first team. Neil had run a successful youth team. A former Scottish international, he was still fit enough in his forties to turn out for the reserves and, though a hard taskmaster, he had the respect of his players. Results of his reserve and youth teams spoke for themselves. Neil left Walsall soon after me and went out of football. This was sad as he had so much to offer.

This was the end of act two at Walsall as far as I was concerned. I hoped that in due course circumstances might change and that there could be an act three, but it was not to be. I could, however, feel proud a season later when players that I had signed, such as Ron Green, Kenny Mower, Brian Caswell, David Preece, Craig Shakespeare and Mark Rees, were in the Walsall side that reached the Milk Cup semi-final and drew 2-2 with Liverpool at Anfield in the first leg in February 1984. I certainly didn't realise at that time that more than twenty years of scouting lay before me and that none of them would be at Walsall.

# FIVE

# HAPPY DAYS AT SHREWSBURY TOWN

*A player who is one-footed is not necessarily a bad player. He can only use one foot at a time.*

*Experienced scouts are invaluable. Quality not quantity is what counts.*

The saying that as one door closes another opens came true for me when, just days after I had left Walsall early in March 1981, I became Shrewsbury Town's chief scout. I had met their player-manager Graham Turner many times while I was working for Walsall. After playing for Chester and Wrexham he had joined Shrewsbury, initially as a player, in 1973. In 1978 he had been appointed manager in succession to Richie Barker, but he had continued to play in their defence and in 1979 he had led them to promotion to the old Second Division for the first time in their history. Whenever I met Graham at games (at some of which we were the only visitors) it became clear from our conversations that we were looking for the same qualities in players. From time to time he had said that he was finding the triple responsibilities of scouting, taking training and playing himself to be increasingly demanding and that if I ever fancied a change of club I should contact him. Thus I found myself meeting Graham at the Spread Eagle on the A5 soon after leaving Walsall, and he fixed up the meeting at Trentham with Shrewsbury chairman

Tim Yates, as described near the beginning of this book. I had no hesitation in accepting the position of chief scout at Shrewsbury and on the day that I handed in my club car to Walsall, Shrewsbury delivered one to me.

Right from the start I found Shrewsbury to be an efficient and yet homely club and I warmed to the friendship of the four people with whom I was to work most closely. Chairman Tim Yates was a typical genial English country gentleman, player-manager Graham Turner was an inspirational motivator and secretary Mal Starkey, who had played in 140 first-team games and scored 18 goals for Shrewsbury between 1959 and 1963 was always co-operative and eager to please. Fourth but not least, Joan Fox, Mal's assistant, was a tremendous support behind the scenes. Her husband was the club electrician. Sadly he is no longer with us, but as this book is being written Joan is still working part-time at Shrewsbury, a most knowledgeable and dedicated football fan, a really charming lady. I was immediately made to feel part of the furniture at Shrewsbury and when I joined them they were in their third ever season in the old Second Division. Of their playing staff I was interested to see Chic Bates, who came from West Bromwich, still doing well up front. I had tried to sign him for Walsall in his Stourbridge days. He had moved to Shrewsbury in 1974, to Swindon in 1978 and had returned to Shrewsbury in 1980.

Whereas in my latter time at Walsall I had seemed to be fighting daily battles, at Shrewsbury I seemed to be appreciated right from the start. Maybe I was lucky but just as at Walsall where I had signed Colin Taylor, one of the club's greatest ever goal-scorers, within weeks of my appointment as chief scout, I managed to sign one of Shrewsbury's best ever defenders soon after landing at the Gay Meadow. The player was Nigel Pearson, whom I saw playing for Heanor Town during Nigel Clough's time as a player there. Nigel Pearson was in his last year at grammar school and I was immediately impressed with his heading ability and leadership qualities. I contacted the Heanor manager and secured his permission for Nigel to play a couple of games for Shrewsbury reserves. The first of these was at Chester and Graham and I met up at the Little Chef at Prees Heath on the A41 and travelled together to the game. Nigel did well enough for Graham to confirm my enthusiasm for this young defender, and he was signed within days. By the start of the following season (1982/83) Nigel was playing regularly at the heart of the Shrewsbury defence, often with Graham (still holding his own as a player at the age of thirty-five) alongside him. Nigel's first two seasons at Shrewsbury coincided with the club's highest ever positions of ninth and eighth respectively in the Second Division. By the time he moved on to Sheffield Wednesday in 1987 he had played in 186 first-team games and the fee of half a million pounds that Wednesday paid for him was a far cry from the reputed fee of £500 plus a friendly game that was paid initially.

It was early in my days at Shrewsbury that I strengthened the link with a certain Harry Maney, a school caretaker in Smethwick who ran a team called Newton Albion. While at Walsall I had signed Don Penn and Paul Waddington from this source and one of the early signings for Shrewsbury was Mark Taylor, a player equally happy in midfield or defence. He did not stay long at the Gay Meadow at this stage and actually made his Football League debut for Walsall in 1984, later returning to Shrewsbury via Sheffield Wednesday and playing nearly 300 games for them. Mark was still active with Redditch as a player-coach in 2004. Other players who came to Shrewsbury from Newton Albion in my early days at the Gay Meadow were Andy Kerr, a central defender with distinctive dreadlocks, twin strikers Gerry Nardiello and Karl Foster, and midfielder Martin Myers. Foster later went to America, joined a band and did not return, while Myers went to Telford and was still playing in the Doc Martens League in 2004. Nor must we forget Carlton Palmer, a tall, very fit young player, strong in the tackle and possessed of a good engine. He later won 18 full England caps but his time at Shrewsbury was cut short by a brush with the manager.

Another player who, like Nigel Pearson, quickly progressed to the Shrewsbury first team was Colin Robinson. I had first seen him playing in an Inter-League game in Birmingham for the Campbell Orr Shield. Later I saw him playing for Mile Oak (the Tamworth club that was so often a happy hunting ground for me) and he impressed me with his speed and heading ability. I signed him in November 1982 and in February 1983 he scored on his first-team debut after going on as a substitute for Bernard McNally. He went on to score 53 goals in 273 games for Shrewsbury before moving to Birmingham in 1988 and Hereford in 1989, though sadly injury blighted his later career. He was a real 100 per cent player and a most likeable personality. Colin played numerous times in the same Shrewsbury first team as Gary Hackett. This lively winger was playing for Bromsgrove when I first recognised Football League potential in him. He was signed for a month's trial period in 1983. Graham was initially uncertain whether to offer him a more permanent contract, but then Gary had an excellent game against Leicester reserves on the technical college ground. This was a game that Graham and I watched together one Saturday morning before seeing the first team in the afternoon, and it ended any doubts Graham may have had about signing Gary on a more permanent basis. Gary made his first-team debut on the opening day of the 1983/84 season and in the course of 183 games for Shrewsbury he operated successfully on either wing, was an excellent crosser of the ball and scored a memorable goal in an FA Cup tie against Ipswich. He moved to Aberdeen in 1987 and later played for a variety of clubs, including West Bromwich Albion and Stoke. At the time of writing he is joint manager of Stourbridge.

Graham and I signed another winger at the same time as Gary Hackett. This was Paul Tester, whom we watched incognito after paying for admission to see him in the Cheltenham team in an evening game in their pre-Football League days. I was always looking for left-footed players to give balance to a side and Paul had a delightful left foot. He had real pace and had scored 25 goals for Cheltenham in the 1982/83 season. It took him a little longer to establish himself in the Shrewsbury team, but he went on to play 129 games in his five seasons, most of them as a left-flank attacker or as a wing-back before this became a regularly accepted position. He later had two good seasons with Hereford.

While Gary and Paul were signed almost immediately as professionals, another winger, Tim Steele, was signed at a younger age as an apprentice after doing well in schoolboy football. He played for Nuneaton Schools and Warwickshire Schools, for both of whom Roger Jacques was secretary. I remember seeing him play in a game at Burton-upon-Trent in the shadow of the cooling towers. Soon afterwards, Graham and I met both his parents (who were separated) and signed him as an apprentice. By the time Tim signed as a professional in December 1985 Graham and I had moved on, but we met up with Tim again when, after 68 games for Shrewsbury, he signed for Wolves for a modest fee in February 1989.

Not all of the signings in which I was involved played regularly for the first team. Defender Kevin Collins was signed from Boldmere

St Michaels in January 1984 when Graham was out of town, and it was chairman Tim Yates who agreed to the signing of this left-sided player. He played only one first-team game for Shrewsbury (at Cardiff in March 1984) but I later signed him for Derby and this splendidly reliable player later had spells at Hereford and Kidderminster, and is now running his own business. Another player who I signed for two different clubs was goalkeeper Ron Green, who had signed for me at Walsall in 1977 and joined me at Shrewsbury in the summer of 1984, succeeding Steve Ogrizovic after the latter's move to Coventry. Ron played for half a season before moving to Bristol Rovers but, by this time, the situation at Shrewsbury had become complicated by Graham's move to take charge of Aston Villa in the summer of 1984. Graham's successes at Shrewsbury had not gone unnoticed and he had had a number of approaches from bigger clubs before he agreed to take up Aston Villa chairman Doug Ellis's offer to succeed Tony Barton, who had led Villa to European Cup success in 1982 but had since suffered ill health. Graham asked me to join him at Villa Park but I did not think that this was the time for me to take a full-time job in football, which would necessitate me retiring from my teaching career. Nor did I feel that Graham was quite ready for the type of challenge that managing Aston Villa presented. He and I had often talked of the possibility of moving to a 'sleeping giant' kind of club if the offer came along, but while Villa were at that time a giant as far as football was concerned, they were certainly not sleeping and were hungry for continuous success. To me it seemed that this was the right club at the wrong time and though Graham spent many hours at my house trying to get me to change my mind, I was adamant.

Such was my relationship with Graham that I sought permission from Shrewsbury Town's chairman to try to get him to change his mind. I even rang him while he was on a Mediterranean cruise, but his heart was set on what he saw a promotion to an obviously bigger job, and my persuasive powers failed to move him. Thus our happy and successful partnership that had lasted for three years was over, at least for the time being.

I thus began the 1984/85 season still at Shrewsbury, but with Chic Bates in charge. Chic followed in the footsteps of Maurice Evans, Alan Durban, Richie Barker and Graham Turner in being appointed Shrewsbury manager from within the club. I had always rated Chic as an honest player and a useful goalscorer, and he was still playing when he took over a side that had finished in the top ten in the old Second Division in both the previous seasons. The new season began quietly with moderate results. Life went on at this happy little club, but such is fate that within three months I was presented with another opportunity in football. This led to me leaving Shrewsbury Town with some happy memories of my time there, working alongside such excellent people. I shall always remember my three-and-a-half seasons there with affection. I had made some good signings and I had the highest regard not only for the players and officials of the club, but also for the fans whose expectations were based on common sense rather than pie in the sky and who were at that time savouring the most successful spell in the club's history. The atmosphere at the club was always pleasant and relaxed, reflecting the town itself. I know that the Turner family also enjoyed their time there.

# SIX

# DERBY COUNTY – AND MY FIRST FULL-TIME APPOINTMENT IN FOOTBALL

*Goals that are match-winners are more valuable than goals in a 7-1 win.*

*Information is strength.*

It was early in the 1984/85 season after I had worked for a few weeks alongside Chic Bates at Shrewsbury that I received a phone call from Arthur Cox, who was in his first season as manager at Derby County. Arthur's playing career had been ended in his late teens while with Coventry City, and he became one of the youngest first-team coaches when he joined Walsall in his mid-twenties. I was then chief scout at Fellows Park and Arthur and I became close friends. He stayed with me for a short time after the tragic death of his first wife. Then, soon after he had joined Tommy Docherty at Villa Park in 1968, he and Tommy approached me over a meal at Perry Barr to become Aston Villa's chief scout. I did not feel that the time was right for such a move at that time. It would have been a full-time post and, at that time, at the age of forty, I was happy working part-time for Walsall while continuing my career in education. During discussions, however, I had been both amazed and amused by Tommy Docherty's infectious enthusiasm. He must have upped his offer four or five times during our hour-long conversation.

Arthur was Bob Stokoe's assistant at Sunderland when they won the FA Cup in 1973. He had then managed Chesterfield from 1976 to 1980 and Newcastle from 1980 to 1984, taking them to promotion from the old Second Division in his last season there. Now he was in charge at Derby, who had just been relegated to the Third Division for only the second time in their history, and he was keen for me to join him on a full-time basis. I was thus faced with the same dilemma that I had faced a few months earlier when Graham Turner had asked me to join him at Villa Park. I was, at the time, well established as head teacher of Mesty Croft School, Wednesbury and, after lengthy discussions with Arthur and Derby chairman Stuart Webb at the Riverside Hotel in Burton-upon-Trent, it was finally agreed that I should work part-time at Derby for the rest of the 1984/85 season. I would then take early retirement from Mesty Croft in the summer of 1985 and become full-time chief scout for Derby County. This would be something of a wrench after almost twenty-five years (almost half of my life up to that point) at Mesty Croft, the last eighteen as head teacher.

Though there was little money available at Derby, Arthur soon gave the team a more purposeful look. I saw at first hand the clarity of his thinking as he sought a right-flank attacker. Evidence was collected of possible players such as Gary Hackett, whom I had taken to Shrewsbury, and Ian Holloway, the present-day manager of QPR. Then the name of Gary Micklewhite came up. He was at that time playing for QPR and Arthur ultimately decided that Micklewhite was the player to go for, as he scored more goals than either Hackett or Holloway and several of these goals turned out to be match-winners in single-goal victories. Arthur would often look at a team on paper (other teams as well as his own) and count up the goal potential. As he quite rightly said, it is goals that win matches.

Another signing soon after my arrival at Derby was that of Geraint Williams, whom Arthur secured from Bristol Rovers just before the transfer deadline in March 1985. Geraint had been watched by several of the staff at Derby and was clearly a busy and honest competitor who liked to win. Arthur always liked players used to winning and this was reflected in the signings he made. Soon Derby were on the up Three wins and two draws in the last five games lifted them to a final position of seventh in the Third Division.

I now found myself, in the summer of 1985, saying goodbye to teaching after thirty-eight years and taking my first full-time job in soccer at the age of fifty-six. I left my full-time post in education on Friday 20 July 1985 and began full-time work with Derby County on the following Monday. I still have vivid memories of my final assembly. The children filed from the hall class by class, leaving me alone with the music teacher Janet Jones. She put down the piano lid, picked up her music and walked out of the hall. My eyes were wet and I found myself alone with one outstanding thought, namely 'You silly fool. You have just willingly given up the best and most rewarding job in the world seven years before you need have done.' I loved my job, loved my school, almost a brand new school, which I had opened on the old site three years earlier after fighting hand-in-hand with parents to have the old one replaced. Yes, I clearly remembered when I lobbied with parents outside West Bromwich Town Hall to get the building of the new Mesty Croft right at the top of the new building programme. We won. The new Mesty Croft stands now as evidence and I am proud of it. Many people had helped me, including local MP Betty Boothroyd, the future Speaker of the House of Commons, who visited me at Mesty Croft to establish the facts.

At that time I did not realise what effect my change in employment would have and it took me some time to adjust to my new responsibilities and my new way of life (including the A38 to Derby). In these early days I thought with affection of the hundreds, indeed thousands, of children who had passed through my hands. I thought of the sports days I'd organised, the plays and pantomimes I had produced, the swimming galas I had arranged and the Parent-Teachers Association I had formed. All these and their accompanying rewards were vivid memories. Life had been very full. There had been no time to stand and stare and I had not wanted to. Success had been my main aim, both in the academic and sporting spheres.

Alongside my teaching career I had served first as treasurer of the Wednesbury branch of the NUT and then as secretary of the Sandwell branch of the NUT. I had represented the local branches at National Conferences. I had also served as a West Bromwich magistrate from 1975 to 1989. As they say, 'If you want a job doing ask a busy man.' I was busy and would not have wanted to be anything else. Now the new focus of my life was Derby County.

While working part-time for the club, I had been impressed by the fact that just about everybody working for Derby County was a keen supporter and every job at the club was done by someone who was both capable and enthusiastic. The chairman, manager and secretary each had their own secretary and I was lucky to have the secretarial services of Marion Taylor, who in more recent times has married former Derby player Ted McMinn, who, sad to say, died recently. She was a tower of strength, reliability personified. She is now club secretary and I still keep in contact with her.

There was also an impressive number of scouts working for Derby County at that time and I was given the authority to review them and to retain those that I wished to. In the event most of them were kept on and happily they were scattered over various parts of the country, something I had not known at my previous clubs. There were strong links at Derby with former players and during my time there those operating as scouts included a number of well-known names, most of whom were in between jobs. Ex-Derby players who scouted at times for me included Bruce Rioch, David Nish and Henry Newton, while Graham Turner also scouted for Derby for a short time after leaving Aston Villa in 1986. So did Don Dorman, after ending his long association with Birmingham City. Rarely have I come across such a dedicated group of scouts, none more efficient than Ken Guttridge, who was the epitome of all that is good in a scout, whatever the weather. Other Derby scouts who served the club splendidly included Phil Waller and Maurice Edwards.

One less positive aspect of the scouting of Derby County, however, was the fact that promising young players from schools in Derbyshire did not automatically link up with Derby County, and I sought to improve this situation by inviting schools within the county one by one to first-team games, allocating them free tickets. This brought them into line with schools in the City of Derby that had long been linked with the club. Thanks to the efficiency of Marion Taylor, each school association knew well in advance to which game they were coming.

Maybe I was lucky but, as had happened at both Walsall and Shrewsbury, I managed to make a more-than-useful signing within a few weeks of my appointment at Derby. The player was Phil Gee, a painter and decorator by trade, who by a remarkable coincidence lived at Pelsall, within a few miles of my Walsall home. I had received a tip from Roy McFarland, Derby's assistant manager, that former Derby defender David Nish, who was a publican in that area, had said that it might be worth my while to watch Gresley Rovers. No particular player was mentioned to me and I went over to Gresley for an evening game on August Bank Holiday Monday after watching Macclesfield in the afternoon. I soon realised that the player David Nish almost certainly had in mind was Phil Gee, a striker with pace, all-round skills and an eye for goal. I realised that other scouts were watching and so I left the ground just before half-time, and was devious enough to say goodbye to those near me as if I had no further interest in the game. In fact I drove home in time to ring Gresley manager Frank Norwood at the end of the game, but before any other scouts descended. He was surprised that I was not still at the ground as he had seen me during the first half. I told Frank of my interest in Phil Gee and he gave me time to ring Derby chairman Stuart Webb before doing anything else. Stuart immediately said 'Get things moving.' To cut a long story short, I picked up Phil Gee the following morning, took him to Derby and completed the signing. On the very next day, Phil made his reserve-team debut against Everton reserves and within minutes he had scored. What's more he got 31 goals in 28 games that season as Derby reserves romped to the Central League title. In due course he got 25 goals in 199 first-team games before moving to Leicester. Thus I had got off to a good start as a full-time chief scout, happy to have made a good signing and to realise that I had the full backing of the club.

Roy McFarland was then in charge of Derby reserves and he fully endorsed Arthur Cox's policy of building a strong reserve side from experienced players, rather than using it just to help bring on young players. Thus any young players being brought in would be helped by the fact that they were coming into a successful side. Like Arthur Cox, Roy liked winners. I thus found myself seeking to sign not only players who would hopefully become first-team regulars, but also players who would play mainly in the reserves but who could be expected to put up a reasonable show when called on for the first team. Thus, while I was pleased to recommend the signing of Micky Forsyth from West Bromwich Albion in March 1985 and to take pleasure in the fact that he played in 92 games in two seasons, I was also happy to recommend defender Kevin Collins from Shrewsbury. Though he never actually played in the Derby first team, he was a key figure in the reserve team's defence in their Central League championship season.

Soon after joining Derby I started to watch non-League teams in the Derbyshire area, such as Heanor and Worksop. I already had happy memories of Heanor as I had signed Nigel Pearson for Shrewsbury from there in 1981. It was while watching Heanor in 1985 that I first saw striker David Penney playing for Pontefract Colliery. David played mainly as a substitute for Derby, but moved on to play over 100 games each for Oxford and Swansea, and then had a useful season with Cardiff. He has since twice taken Doncaster to promotion, having initially linked up with them in their Conference days. I well remember walking into Roy McFarland's office the morning after signing David Penney and Roy commenting that by my demeanour he knew I had made a signing.

Another player signed during my first season as full-time chief scout of Derby County was Hartlepool defender David Linighan. I recall the dash up to Hartlepool to have a second look at David one Saturday morning in 1986. I had already seen him on the previous Friday evening in a game at Stockport and on the Saturday morning a week later I went to Walsall's Fellows Park to meet up with Ken Guttridge, who had travelled there with Derby's third team. Before half-time in this Walsall reserves *v.* Derby 'A' game, Ken and I left for Hartlepool. Ken still talks of the selection of sandwiches and drinks that I took to sustain us on the long journey. This was another game at which we paid to enter the ground so that our intentions were not revealed to possible rivals for Linighan's signature, although one or two fans did recognise us. David Linighan did not actually make the first team at Derby but, after half a season in the reserves, he moved on to play for a season and a half for Shrewsbury before going on to play over 300 times for Ipswich and over 100 times for Blackpool. It can be said, therefore, that I inadvertently scouted for other clubs who took on a player whose talent I had first recognised.

The strong Derby reserve side, which in 1985/86 became the first reserve side of a Third Division club ever to win the Central League title, was a major factor in Derby's first team winning promotion to the old Second Division in 1986 and to the old First Division in 1987. During this time Arthur Cox both bought and sold well, most signings being the result of gathering together a number of opinions on possible recruits. He also put a high priority on players accustomed to winning, whether it be in the Derby reserve side or for other clubs. A typical example of the latter was Steve McClaren, who was signed from Hull in the summer of 1985 after helping the Tigers to win promotion from the Third Division. A consummate professional, Steve was ever-present in his first two seasons at Derby, in both of which promotion was won, so that Steve himself was actually in a promotion-winning side in three successive seasons. Steve later joined Bristol City and Oxford before returning to Derby as a coach and then moving on to serve both Manchester United and England as assistant manager, taking on his first managerial appointment at Middlesbrough in 2001.

A few months after the signing of McClaren, Derby's midfield was further strengthened by the signing of John Gregory from QPR. John was an influential player with good skills and in the course of his 25 games for Derby he was clearly learning the trade that was to see him become a manager at a comparatively early age. John spent hours in my office talking and making notes in a notebook that he carried everywhere with him. He was determined to succeed in the game, wanting to be a good captain and ultimately a successful manager. I liked him and we got on very well.

I took particular pleasure in the signing of goalkeeper Mark Wallington from Leicester in the summer of 1985. I had first signed him for Walsall fourteen years earlier and on both occasions he was secured at a bargain price. Another bargain signing around that time was winger Jeff Chandler from Bolton. He had been watched on many occasions before being signed, and he proved well worth the £38,000 that was the price fixed by a tribunal. He scored twice on his debut against Bournemouth on the opening day of the 1985/86 season and in a second round FA Cup tie got a hat-trick against Telford. In addition to the goals that he scored, his skill on the ball made him a great crowd pleaser.

Then there were the useful reserve players, such as goalkeeper Martin Taylor from Tamworth side Mile Oak Rovers. Rovers again proved a happy hunting ground for me. Martin was a miner by trade who played just over 100 first-team games in ten years with Derby and went on to have six good years with Wycombe, having been signed by former Derby man John Gregory. Eighteen years after signing him for Derby I signed Martin again – this time as goalkeeping coach and cover goalkeeper for Telford United. Incidentally, Martin first made a name in the Derby dressing room when a Derby County cricket team were short of an opening batsman for a Sunday game during pre-season training. Martin, who as he said 'played a bit', filled the vacancy and scored a big hundred, really looking the part of a county cricketer.

Arthur Cox's concern to develop young players can be gathered from the fact that he and I agreed to sign up to ten YTS players, and among those I signed were defender Scott Green (another player destined to link up with me again at Telford years later), defender Stuart Edwards from Walsall and midfielder Craig Ramage, who later won England Under-21 caps and did well for Watford and Bradford City. Unfortunately for Derby, Rufus Brevett failed to get into the team and was passed on to Doncaster, from where he went on to do well for Watford and Fulham. I had just over two-and-a-half good years as chief scout at Derby, but the flip side of my first experience of full-time work in soccer was that the journey up and down the A38 added two-and-a-half hours to each working day.

Meanwhile, things were happening nearer home at Molineux. Two Shropshire gentlemen, Jack Harris and Dick Homden, who had been on the Walsall board for part of my time there, were now Wolves directors and had just appointed Graham Turner as manager. I had of course worked with Graham at Shrewsbury in the early 1980s and Messrs Harris and Homden saw a renewal of the Turner-Jukes partnership as the way forward for a Wolves team who had just suffered relegation in three successive seasons to land up in the Fourth Division for the first time. It was an attractive prospect for me to cut down on travelling and to join a club for whom I had played as a junior. On the other hand I had no quarrel with Derby County, who had treated me very well, and I realised that if I moved to Wolves I would be exchanging the best-organised club I had experienced for one in desperate financial straits and rumoured to have a bucket catching the water that descended from a hole in the roof. Arthur Cox was not happy at the prospect of my leaving Derby and I felt regret at leaving a manager for whom I had the greatest respect. Arthur was the personification of punctuality and discipline but with a real concern for people. I remembered the way he had challenged a young player who had seemed reluctant to clean the toilets. Arthur asked the youth who cleaned the toilet at home. When he replied that his mother did, Arthur's immediate riposte was 'If it's good enough for your mother, then it's good enough for you. Get it done.'

Another vivid memory of working with Arthur was when, mid-afternoon one day, he asked me to travel to Bournemouth to see goalkeeper David Felgate playing for Lincoln that evening. 'Take Ken Hodgkisson with you to help with the driving,' he added. When I contacted and picked up 'Hodgy' he mentioned that Northampton were about to sign defender Mick Forsyth from West Bromwich Albion where he (Hodgy) still had links. Knowing that Derby were interested in Forsyth I immediately rang Arthur from a call box. He moved quickly and signed Forsyth. As it turned out I did not recommend David Felgate, though he was a useful goalkeeper, and a long day ended with a dense fog over Salisbury Plain on the return journey, which lasted well into the night.

When the time came Arthur did, however, agree reluctantly for me to move from Derby to Wolves since the excessive travelling was putting undue strain on my health. We have continued to contact each other regularly since this parting of the ways as Arthur has furthered his experience, which has included working alongside Kevin Keegan at Fulham, for England and at Manchester City. As this book was being written he announced his retirement, though I cannot imagine that his dynamic character will sit at home in his slippers for long.

Once again I was leaving behind many good friends, including Derby secretary Michael Dunford, who later moved to Everton as chief executive. I could, however, feel happy that during my time at Derby I had played my part in transforming a Third Division team into one pressing for promotion for the second successive season and with a strong reserve team.

# SEVEN

# TO WOLVES IN 1986

*Play to your strengths. Avoid your weaknesses.*

*You can please some of the people all of the time. You can please all of the people some of the time. You can't please all of the people all of the time.*

Though I had declined to join Graham Turner when he took over at Aston Villa in 1984 and invited me to follow him from Shrewsbury, I felt that it was the right move just over two years later when I was invited to become his chief scout at Wolves. I was now available to work in a full-time capacity, having retired from my post in education when becoming chief scout of Derby County in July 1985. Despite the fact that Derby were on their way to a second successive promotion season and Wolves were struggling in the Fourth Division, there was a great attraction for me in joining a club just eight miles from my home and whom I had supported as a boy when I had watched Walsall and Wolves on alternate Saturdays, cycling to the games and paying two old pence for my cycle to be stored during the game. Such was my enthusiasm that when neither first team was at home I watched the reserves.

As previously mentioned, when Graham and I were working together at Shrewsbury we had talked of one day moving to a club with great potential who were going through difficult times. Now it seemed that this opportunity had presented itself right on our respective doorsteps. Wolves had been the top British club for much of the 1950s, winning three League Championships in the space of six years and beating top European club sides Spartak Moscow, Honved and Real Madrid in those legendary floodlit friendly games when the European Cup and the Champions' League were still only faint twinkles in football administrators' eyes. In 1986, however, Wolves were in the Fourth Division and struggling for their very existence. They had kicked off the 1986/87 season with 4 defeats in their first 7 games and stories abounded of unpaid bills and a ground literally falling apart in places. I did, however, look forward to rediscovering the rapport that I had shared with Graham at Shrewsbury. What's more, there were some loyal staff still around at Molineux. For instance Keith Pearson, who had joined the club in 1975, initially as an accountant, was a most friendly personality, thoroughly enjoyed his job and was loyalty personified, as he seemed to will the club to do well. Then there was Dot Wooldridge, who finally retired in 2004 while this book was being written. She had worked behind the scenes longer than most people could remember. The whole philosophy of the club at this time was later to be expressed by Graham Turner in the title of his book *The Only Way is Up*.

My first task after appointment was to get together a team to fulfil an FA Youth Cup fixture that was waiting to be played. Wolves lost the game but at least we managed to get together a team to fulfil the fixture. Then, just to remind everyone of the dire state the club was in, the first team lost to Chorley in a twice-replayed FA Cup tie. Before that infamous Chorley tie, however, I had been involved in the signing of two players who were to play a major part in the destiny of Wolves over the next few years and one of whom was to become Wolves' record goalscorer of all time.

Right from the start of my scouting career I had been a regular attender at reserve-team games in the Midlands, and when news was released that West Bromwich Albion were eager to offload some of a rather unwieldy playing staff I immediately thought of the Tipton-born striker Steve Bull, who had the heart of a lion in his quest for goals, and cultured defender Andy Thompson. Graham Turner immediately backed me in my desire to sign these two players, but our initial approaches to Albion fell on deaf ears. We persisted, however, and eventually a third or fourth phone call to Albion manager Ron Saunders got a positive response. Soon Steve and Andy were coming over to Molineux for transfer talks. It took Steve only a few minutes to decide to sign for Wolves and Andy only a little longer. I have particularly vivid memories of Graham and I going over to The Hawthorns later in the day to get the signatures of Albion officials on the transfer forms. When I met up with the Albion chairman he light-heartedly accused me of getting a 'steal'. Some years later I was at an Albion reserve game in an almost deserted directors' box when I was recognised by a steward who was himself an ex-pupil of mine. He referred to me as 'the bastard who signed Bully'. I felt proud not just to have signed Steve Bull but also to have given one of my pupils such an appropriate command of the English language.

Both Steve and Andy had, in fact, been signed around the time of the Wolves v. Chorley FA Cup tie, which stretched to three games, but they were not signed in time to play in any of these. It took Steve, however, only two games to open his Wolves account in a 1-0 win at Cardiff in a Freight Rover Trophy game on 2 December 1986. One wonders how many Wolves in the meagre 1,201 gate at Ninian Park are reading this. I have been rather amused over recent years to hear many of Wolves' current 25,000 gates claiming that they were watching Wolves in those Chorley days.

Soon the missing fans began to come out of the woodwork as a new era was clearly dawning. By the end of that 1986/87 season Steve Bull had clocked up 19 goals in 37 games while Andy Thompson had become something of a penalty king, most of his 8 goals by the end of that season being from the spot. In the last three months of that season Bull and Thompson had been joined at Molineux by another West Bromwich Albion man, winger Robbie Dennison. Robbie went on to win 18 full Northern Ireland caps and to score a spectacular goal in Wolves' 1988 Sherpa Van Trophy final win over Burnley. Between them, Bull, Thompson and Dennison went on to play a total of 1,365 games for Wolves with Steve becoming the first player in the history of the club to score over 300 goals. Again, as at Walsall, Shrewsbury and Derby, I had been lucky to have had a hand in significant signings within a few weeks of arriving at a new club.

Another product of my regular attendance at Midlands clubs' reserve games was Robert Kelly from Leicester, who played in Wolves' last thirteen games of the 1986/87 season but was then struck down by an

injury that ultimately brought an end to his playing career. When looking for players I have always endeavoured to seek character as well as
ability and here was a young man with real character. He battled bravely
against his injury problems and actually made two substitute appearances
in Wolves' Third Division side after making a partial recovery. When it
became clear, however, that his playing career was over, he went to college to train for a career in journalism in which he worked for a short
time. Then, when he showed an interest in coaching, Graham and I were
delighted for him to rejoin the staff at Molineux as a coach. During
this time he also accompanied me on a number of scouting expeditions.
I particularly remember trips to Scotland to watch Morton's Derek
McInnes (later to join West Bromwich Albion) and Motherwell's Philip
O'Donnell (who later went to Celtic). During these long journeys
Robert was eager to learn details of how to sign players and I appreciated not only his stimulating company but also his readiness to share
the driving. I have been delighted to see how Robert has progressed in
the game and, at the time of writing, he is assistant manager of Leicester
City. Leicester's gain was Wolves' loss, such was Robert's ability to bring
the best out of young players.

I was also grateful during my first season at Wolves for a tip-off from
long-serving *Birmingham Evening Mail* reporter and friend Paul Marston.
He had just watched a Newport County *v.* Walsall game and I asked
about goalkeeper Roger Freestone, whom I'd seen a few weeks before.
When Paul pointed out that Roger was keeping Mark Kendall (a Welsh
Under-21 international in his Spurs days) out of the team I realised
that Mark might be just the man to give that extra bit of security to
the Wolves defence. I knew that he was not just a possessor of a safe
pair of hands, but also a good talker and organiser of his defence. I
really fancied him playing behind Ally Robertson who, after a long and
distinguished career with West Bromwich Albion, was now skippering
Wolves. Mark readily agreed to join Wolves just before Christmas 1986
and in 28 games before the end of the season he kept 15 clean sheets
and the whole defence now had the sort of solid look that I had hoped
for. He then went on to set up a new Wolves record of 28 clean sheets in
1987/88 when they not only topped the Fourth Division but also won
the Freight Rover Trophy. In short, while Steve Bull was scoring goals at

one end Mark Kendall was making sure that not many were conceded at the other. He was, in many ways, the final piece in Wolves' promotion jigsaw and Graham and I were delighted at this most vital signing.

Meanwhile I was also looking at the grass-roots level of the game to make sure that young players of potential were being brought to Molineux. I was backed up by a busy scouting staff operating mainly in the Midlands, with men like Geoff Blackwell and Tony Painter together with Ken Guttridge, who had followed me from Derby. Sometimes, however, young players came from further afield. An example of this was Colin Taylor (no relation to the Walsall player of the same name) a young striker from the Liverpool area whom I first saw playing for a Liverpool team against Wolverhampton Schoolboys in the English Schools' Shield on the Wolverhampton Casuals ground on the Stafford Road. Colin joined Wolves on a YTS scheme and scored a hatful of goals in the reserves and at one time seemed to be the ideal follow-up to Steve Bull. It was disappointing that he ultimately played only 24 first-team games for Wolves and scored just 3 goals, later having loan spells with Preston, Wigan and Doncaster before moving into non-League football with Telford and Runcorn. Wolves also forged close links with North Wales after playing pre-season games against an Anglesey team organised by Chris Evans, a former York City defender whose playing career had been ended by a broken leg. Numerous players came to Wolves from North Wales in the late 1980s, though none actually reached the first team. Chris himself ultimately became youth coach and academy director at Molineux, a position that he still holds as this book goes to press.

Recruiting young players was always to the forefront of Graham Turner's mind. A typical example of a young player recruited locally was Stafford-born Chris Brindley. I had seen him playing for Hednesford as a teenager and also knew him as a useful off-spin bowler. He played just 9 first-team games for Wolves in the late 1980s, but later gave excellent service to Telford and Kidderminster and then, in 2004 at the age of thirty-four, experienced the greatest day of his career when, after returning to his first club Hednesford, he got the match-winner against Canvey Island in the FA Trophy final.

Another young player signed during my early days at Molineux was Paul Grainger, a busy midfielder and yet another useful signing from that great source of talent, Tamworth club Mile Oak Rovers. I had played against Paul's father many years before in junior football and though Paul did not make it to Wolves' first team he was a skilful player who went on to give many years' service to teams such as Stafford and Telford.

At the end of my first season at Molineux it was a great disappointment when Wolves lost to Aldershot in the finals of the 1986/87 Fourth Division promotion play-offs, but it had been a good season overall. Gates had risen from under 4,000 for the visit of Rochdale in November to over 10,000 for the visit of Hereford in April. There were 19,962 at the Aldershot play-off final game against Aldershot. Wolves had ended up 13 points ahead of Aldershot in the Fourth Division and this play-off defeat was bitterly disappointing. Play-offs were, however, thought by most people to be for the good of the game and they certainly stimulated interest in a season for longer and brought in extra revenue. Despite this disappointment we all felt in the summer of 1987 that the corner had been turned at Molineux and the close season gave the opportunity to strengthen a side that in fact went on to win promotion in each of the next two seasons and also to win the Sherpa Van Trophy for good measure. The defence was strengthened by the signing of Gary Bellamy from Chesterfield. He had been in the Spireites' Fourth Division Championship side of 1985 and this was another example of signing a player accustomed to success. Gary was able to play on either the right side of the defence or in the centre and he went on to play 165 games for Wolves then won a Welsh Cup medal with Cardiff City. He then had three good seasons with Leyton Orient and later still managed Dover Athletic, where I have recently come into contact with him again.

In the course of 1987/88 the team was further strengthened by the acquisition of another versatile player, Phil Chard from Northampton, who was equally happy in midfield or defence. Like Bellamy he played for Wolves in three different divisions and, after returning to Northampton, managed the Cobblers for a spell in 1992/93.

A key figure in Wolves' midfield in 1987/88 was tough-tackling Keith Downing, a fair-haired player signed from Notts County during the previous summer. Early in his career he had been one of the numerous players to join Shrewsbury in my time there from Smethwick club Newton Albion, but he did not break through into the Shrewsbury first team. He then linked up with Mile Oak Rovers (yes, that little Tamworth club again) before moving to Notts County in 1984. He was released by County in 1987 and so was a free agent. Accordingly, I telephoned his house only to find that he was on holiday. I left a message for him to contact me on his return. This he did, we met and talked and he signed for Wolves. He went on to play 228 games in Wolves' midfield, his competitive edge earning him the nickname of 'Psycho' from fans. He later linked up with Graham Turner and I at Hereford, returned to Molineux as youth coach in 1989 and at the time of writing is working with former Wolves assistant manager John Ward at Cheltenham. Contrasting in style with Keith Downing was that delicate little midfielder Nigel Vaughan, who arrived at Molineux a month later. He had been in Newport's 1979/80 Fourth Division promotion team and had then moved to Cardiff. I had seen him 'running the show' from midfield in Newport's 4-2 win at Walsall on the final day of that 1979/80 season. He was a skilful, thoughtful player whom I always thought was undervalued. In 2004 he was coaching at Shrewsbury. He actually made his Wolves debut in September 1987 against his former club Cardiff, scored a goal and a few weeks later netted 5 times in 8 games to show that he was not just a skilful ball player. He too served in Wolves' successive promotion wins and he too later rejoined Graham Turner at Hereford.

Not all of our signings for Wolves in 1987 made such an immediate impact, but most of them proved to be well worthwhile in the end. I had watched Phil Robinson in the Aston Villa reserve team for some time and was about to sign him as a versatile player, equally happy in midfield or defence. Then Villa manager Billy McNeill departed and his successor Graham Taylor hesitated about letting the deal go through. Eventually a small fee was agreed upon and Phil went on to play 90 games for Wolves. Then, after joining Notts County, he was loaned to Birmingham in time to play in their Leyland DAF Cup-winning team in 1991. He was another player who ultimately rejoined Graham Turner at Hereford, where he served as both player and coach before being released and going on to manage his home-town club Stafford Rangers.

Fair-haired defender Mark Venus cost rather more than the modest fee paid for Phil Robinson but he proved well worth the £40,000 paid to Leicester City in March 1988. I had first seen Mark in the very strong

Leicester reserve side when I was scouting for Derby. He had often played in the same side as Robert Kelly, whom we took to Molineux exactly a year before Mark. He went on to help Ipswich back into the Premiership in 2000 and to win a place in Europe a year later. While this book was being written I received a phone call from Mark saying that he had been offered a coaching job with Scottish club Hibernian. He asked me to join him. I declined.

As Wolves were strengthened for what turned out to be highly success-ful 1987/88 season we must not forget good squad players such as Jackie Gallagher, who had seen service with Lincoln, Torquay and Peterborough and had also played in Hong Kong before landing up at Molineux. He was useful cover for Steve Bull and Andy Mutch and, in the course of two seasons, more than half his 36 appearances were as substitute, one of them in the Sherpa Van Trophy final of 1988.

After the winning of the Fourth Division championship and the Sherpa Van Trophy in 1988 the question was what extra resources were needed if Wolves were to make an immediate challenge for promo-tion from the old Third Division in 1988/89. Behind the scenes Barry Powell, who had figured in Wolves' 1974 League Cup-winning team, joined the coaching staff and Paul Darby took over as physiotherapist. Initially the Fourth Division championship side was given the chance to show what it could do in the Third Division and they responded well, with two wins and a draw in their first four games. At this time I was very keen on Mick Gooding and was delighted when he was signed from Peterborough for a reported £80,000. He quickly settled into the right side of midfield, playing in the whole of the twelve-game unbeaten run around the turn of the year that brought promotion for the second time in two seasons within Wolves' grasp. After just a season and a half Mick moved on to spend nearly eight years with Reading, in the course of which he had a spell as joint-manager. More recently he has been youth coach at Walsall. Two goalkeepers came on loan in the course of 1988/89, Roger Hansbury from Birmingham and Mike Stowell, a very impressive reserve from Everton. Roger kept 3 clean sheets in 6 games for Wolves while Mike, though he did not have such an impressive record during his loan spell, signed on a more permanent basis in 1990 and went on to set an all-time Wolves record by clocking

up a tally of 448 first-team games. At the time of writing Mike is with
Bristol City and we frequently chat together, with Mike keeping me up
to date with players in that area.

Not only did Wolves top the Third Division in 1988/89, but they
picked up 2 more points and scored 14 more goals than they had done in
the Fourth Division in the previous season. Another happy aspect of the
season was that gates rose to an average of 14,330, with 22,352 to see the
semi-final second leg of the Sherpa Van Trophy, which Wolves unfortunately lost to Torquay after dominating most of the game. Former Wolves
man Dean Edwards, who had been released by Graham, got one of the
Torquay goals and after scoring gave Graham the appropriate signal.

Before the end of that 1988/89 season Wolves' first-team squad had
been further strengthened by the signing of Tim Steele from Shrewsbury.
Graham and I had signed him for Shrewsbury in 1985 and he had
performed with distinction for them. By the time we approached him
with a view to joining Wolves he was about to join Notts County. We
persuaded him to think the matter over during a weekend, however,
and we were pleased when he decided to join Wolves. He played his
first full game for Wolves in March 1989 and scored a goal in a 6-1 win
over Gillingham. Having secured promotion for the second successive
season the increasing strength of Wolves' first-team squad was such that
Tim was unable to hold down a regular place in the team that began
the 1989/90 season in the Second Division. Neither could John Paskin,
a twenty-six-year-old striker whom I liked and who had followed the
well-trodden path from The Hawthorns to Molineux in the summer
of 1989. Tony Lange, who had played in the Aldershot goal when they
beat Wolves in the 1987 play-off final, was another close-season signing
but he soon lost his place to Mark Kendall, who was still playing well.
Shane Westley came from Southend and proved to be a powerful figure
at the heart of the defence, although he was not always popular with
fans. Another close-season signing, Paul McLaughlin from Hereford,
failed to make an immediate impact and drifted away. Behind the scenes,
however, Gary Pendrey, who had been brought in as assistant manager,
was making his mark. This former long-serving Birmingham defender
had worked well at Walsall alongside Alan Buckley and had just had
a spell in-charge of his old club Birmingham. His bubbly personality

made him an asset to any dressing room and he still fully participated in five-a-side games. He was a person whom it would be difficult not to like and he commanded the loyalty of the players. He and I became great friends.

Only 5 of the first 14 games of 1989/90 were won and at this stage midfielder Paul Cook was signed from Norwich. I had frequently watched him some years earlier when he was with Wigan and I well remember sitting in the old stand at Springfield Park with my umbrella up in a snowstorm. He had moved to Norwich in 1988 but was not holding down a regular place there. Graham and I went to watch him in a reserve game at Oxford and he seemed to be showing all the qualities that I remembered from his Wigan days – a superb left foot and an outstanding ability to use both the short and the long ball. Next day he was signed and he went straight into Wolves' first team. He went on to play 214 games for them and proved to be well worth the £250,000 fee that was a record for Norwich at the time. He moved to Accrington in 2003. He has kept in touch with me over the years and has an almost encyclopaedic knowledge of Lancashire football.

Wolves ended that 1989/90 season in tenth place in the Second Division and then, during the close season, dramatic changes took place behind the scenes. Wolves fan of many years Sir Jack Hayward bought the club from the Gallaghers and the one and only Billy Wright joined the reconstituted board. Jonathan Hayward, Sir Jack's son, became chairman and a new Molineux was planned, with new stands built on three of the four sides. While this brought great excitement among fans, some did wonder how it would affect the money available for players.

On the field there were major defensive changes. Mike Stowell came from Everton just over a year after his spell on loan and stayed long enough to set a new club appearance record for a goalkeeper. Then Rob Hindmarch, who had skippered Derby County in successive promotion seasons, signed for Wolves after great efforts had been made to sign both him and his defensive partner Paul Blades. They were an excellent partnership, with Rob big and strong and Paul quick and nimble. Paul moved to Norwich, although he did come to Wolves two years later, by which time Hindmarch had moved on. We had learned, not for the first time, that one player on his own is not necessarily half of a successful pair.

When I heard that defender Brian Roberts, the ex-Coventry and Birmingham full-back, had been given a free transfer I phoned him immediately and he thought at first that I was joking when I asked him about joining Wolves. Though in his thirty-fifth year he was still a great battler and capable of playing on either the right or the left side of the defence. A few weeks later a rather younger defender, twenty-one-year-old Kevin Ashley, also came from Birmingham. I had first seen him many years before playing for a Birmingham boys' team and he was with Birmingham City during Dave Mackay's time there as manager. Dave genuinely saw him as a future international but, sadly, he never quite recaptured his Blues' form for Wolves. The crowd never really took to him and this splendidly fast overlapping full-back played only 99 games before moving on to Peterborough in 1994. Kevin was one of several players to suffer injury in that 1990/91 season but a good run just after Christmas raised hopes as Wolves climbed into the top six. Paul Birch (whose brother Alan had signed for Walsall nearly ten years earlier) came from Aston Villa in February and went on to play 166 games for Wolves to add to the 200 he had played for Villa. He brought just the experience that a team needs in midfield. Wolves, however, ended up in twelfth place and it was also disappointing that the reserves, who had climbed to Division One of the Pontins League a year earlier, were now relegated. Young players in the reserves at that time included Paul Jones, a midfielder whom I had previously signed for Walsall and not to be confused with the goalkeeper of the same name. Tom Bennett had come on a free transfer from Aston Villa after impressing me when playing in a Sunday afternoon charity game at Newtown (Wales). He went on to win a regular first-team place and to be Player of the Season in 1991/92. Then there were young strikers Loy Stobart (son of Barry Stobart who had played in Wolves' 1960 FA Cup-winning team), Shaun Bradbury from Telford (who scored twice on his debut against Millwall in May 1993) and for a short time Stan Collymore. I had seen Stan playing for Cannock Police Cadets against Walsall Pegasus at Leamore playing field. He had a great battle with a central defender named Keogh and in fact both were sent off before the end of the game. Both were signed by Walsall, but neither made much progress there. When I heard that Stan had been rejected by Walsall I signed him for Wolves. He played a number of reserve games for Wolves and scored several goals, but was released after a series of brushes with authority. I had, however, seen enough of him to realise what an asset he could be to any side if only he could harness his ability and I remember telling Crystal Palace boss Steve Coppell this when he rang to enquire about him when he was playing for Stafford Rangers. Steve signed Stan and he went on to score over 100 League and cup goals and to win 3 England caps, but one feels that he could have achieved so much more in the game.

A young trainee who was signed around this time was Jamie Smith, who came from Feckenham in the Redditch area. As a sixteen-year-old in 1990 he was a left or right-flank attacker who could score goals. Then one day when Gary Pendrey was struggling to find a right-sided defender to play in a reserve game I suggested that he give Jamie a try. He did well and stayed in that position. Though he didn't get into the first team until after I had left Wolves, Jamie played over 100 games before moving on to Crystal Palace for £900,000. He had a number of good seasons with Palace before injuries led him to being released.

Wolves ended up in twelfth spot in the Second Division in 1990/91 and with relatively few changes in the team they picked up six more points the following season but ended up only one place higher. By this time, however, the ground was beginning to take shape thanks to the vast investments in it made by Sir Jack Hayward. Of the new players in 1991/92 Laurie Madden came from Sheffield Wednesday just one month short of his thirty-sixth birthday. He was still a fine reader of the game and missed only three games in his first season at Molineux. He ultimately became the oldest player ever to appear in Wolves' first team when, at the end of his second season, he turned out in the game at Derby in May 1992 aged thirty-seven years 222 days. He later had a short spell as caretaker manager after the departure of Graham Turner. At the other end of the age range was twenty-two-year-old Mark Rankine, who came from Doncaster in mid-season. He had already captained Rovers and whenever I had seen him he had impressed me with his skill, pace and bubbly personality. He proved to be well worth the reported £70,000 that Wolves paid for him, appearing in defence, midfield and up front in the course of 167 games for Wolves and he then had a successful spell at Preston before joining Tranmere in the summer of 2004.

I was continually trying to strike the balance between keeping the first team supplied with players who were ready to make their mark there immediately and bringing in young players who might ultimately become first-team material. In November 1991 I signed promising young versatile defender Darren Simkin from Blakenall. He ultimately played 16 first-team games and then moved to Shrewsbury. In 2004 he was in the Hednesford team that won the FA Trophy. Then there was goalkeeper Paul Jones. I had remembered his enthusiasm from my Shrewsbury days when he seemed to spend a great deal of time diving about in the mud as a junior trialist. By 1991 he was playing well for Kidderminster in their pre-Football League days and I contacted Harriers manager and long-standing friend Graham Allner and negotiated Paul's transfer to Wolves in a meeting at Penn Cottage on the A449. One of a farming family from Wem, Paul took over from Mike Stowell for a spell in 1992/93 and after 44 games for Wolves went on to join Southampton via Stockport and to do well in the Premiership. He returned to Wolves in 2004 and, at the age of thirty-seven, took his tally of Welsh caps past 40.

February 1992 saw teenage midfielder Jimmy Kelly linking up with Wolves after I had been very impressed by his displays for Wrexham. While he came to Wolves John Paskin moved the other way and Jimmy looked to be a natural successor to Nigel Vaughan in his excellent use of the ball. Sadly he played only a few first-team games for Wolves and, after loan spells with Walsall and back at Wrexham, off-field problems hampered his career though he has, in more recent times, played in the Conference for Chester, Doncaster and Morecambe.

After the successive promotion wins of the late 1980s Wolves reached something of a plateau in the old Second Division in the early 1990s. Players came in and did useful jobs. Paul Blades, for instance, was finally secured from Norwich and formed a useful defensive partnership with Laurie Madden while young striker Darren Roberts, whom I had watched several times playing for Burton Albion, had his moment of glory with a hat-trick on his debut in a Sunday game against Birmingham in September 1992, but after 5 goals in 24 games he moved on to Doncaster and after several more moves ended up at Barrow in 2001. Wolves were holding their own in Division One (as the Second Division had been renamed in 1992) but were not making obvious progress. Fans were becoming restless and this was a good illustration of the fact that no club has the divine right to continuous success. Jonathan Hayward had now been chairman for a couple of years. He had proved himself a great enthusiast and I remember the zeal with which he questioned me during his chats in the boardroom on the subject of regulations regarding transfers whether at grass-roots or Premiership level. He was also very keen to know about rules concerning the signing of schoolboys and the vexed 'seven-day notice' for approaching junior players. He even asked about when 'incentives' could be used and at this stage I ended our chat. At all times he was most eager to learn and his love for Wolves was very apparent.

Wolves ended up in twelfth spot in the renamed Division One in 1992/93 and the following summer we signed Kevin Keen from West Ham. Kevin's father Mike Keen was well known both as a player and manager of QPR, and Kevin was a right-sided midfielder with good pace and excellent vision. At the same time Geoff Thomas came from Crystal Palace into the centre of midfield. Graham and I had watched Geoff in his Crewe days when he had played alongside David Platt and, since then, he had played over 200 games for Crystal Palace. He looked very good in his first eight games for Wolves, but he unfortunately sustained a serious injury in a 2-0 win at Sunderland, in which he got his fourth goal of the season. This injury put him out for the season and extra midfield strength was sought. In January 1994 both Chris Marsden from Huddersfield and Darren Ferguson from Manchester United arrived at Molineux. I had long admired Marsden's left foot and always felt that when he passed the ball he was lending it rather than giving it away. Things looked good when he made his debut in a 2-0 win over Crystal Palace, but sadly he suffered a broken leg a few weeks later and played only 11 games for Wolves. It was a disappointment to me that he stayed only ten months with Wolves, though he has since done well, particularly in his five years with Southampton and at the time of writing he has just retired. I have continued to be a great fan of Chris and it was good to see him captaining Southampton in the 2003 FA Cup final. David Kelly had a purposeful first season with Wolves after having signed from Newcastle in the summer of 1993, getting 14 goals and fitting in quite well alongside Steve Bull, though Bully's total of 15 goals was his lowest in his first eight seasons with Wolves. Vastly experienced striker Cyrille Regis came from Aston

Villa around the same time to complete a tour of Midlands sides, having previously played for West Bromwich Albion and Coventry. At thirty-five he was used mainly as a substitute, but he was an extremely good influence on his fellow professionals, being an extremely pleasant and deeply religious man.

Another striker pressing for a place in that 1993/94 season was Lee Mills. I had first seen Lee playing for Walsall reserves against Wrexham reserves one wet Wednesday evening. He was, in fact, playing in a trial game for Walsall and I had some difficulty in finding out exactly where he had come from. Having heard the vague statement that 'he came down from Sheffield', I contacted a scout I knew in Doncaster and found that he was on the books of a team called Stocksbridge Steel in the Sheffield area in the Unibond League. I decided to watch him in action for this Stocksbridge team and met up with fellow scout Ken Guttridge on the A38. I travelled up with him to Stocksbridge's modest ground that was on high ground but where the gate was only in double figures. By half-time I had been impressed enough by Lee's skills that I found the Stockbridge chairman and manager and got their phone numbers. They told me that Lee was meeting with Coventry on the following Thursday morning and Walsall on the following Thursday afternoon. I told Graham Turner that time was of the essence and arranged for Lee and the Stockbridge manager to have lunch at Molineux after seeing Coventry on the Thursday morning. Graham received them warmly and by the time they had looked round Molineux and chatted freely we had learned that Lee worked as a civil servant in Barnsley and that he would be willing to sign for Wolves. We persuaded him to cancel his meeting with Walsall that afternoon and with nothing having been settled at Coventry in the morning we were free to complete the deal on the following evening when we met up with the Stocksbridge chairman, who had travelled down to Mansfield to meet us. A down payment from Wolves was agreed upon and Lee handed in his notice at work and did well in the short term for Wolves before moving on to Derby, Port Vale, Coventry and Stoke before linking up again with me at Telford in 2003. A year later he was still doing well for Hereford.

There were certainly plenty of players coming to Wolves at this time, but sadly not all initial hopes were realised. A particular disappointment to all was the injury sustained by Neil Masters. This skilful defender had been signed from Bournemouth in December 1993 after Graham and I had watched him in an FA Cup replay at Nuneaton. Fellow scout Geoff Blackwell had queued up to get us tickets for a game that was a potential sell-out. It was a very wet night and Graham and I got a real soaking while standing behind the goals but, even in these conditions, Masters was clearly an outstanding defender. He was well built and had pace and an excellent left foot. Soon he was making his Wolves debut in a 1-1 draw at Tranmere, but he was injured late in that game and was never the same player again. He played just 10 games for Wolves and, after a spell with Gillingham, dropped out of League football altogether. What a tragedy.

What proved to be one of my last signings at Molineux was that of Darren Ferguson, son of Sir Alex. Graham and I had watched him in a reserve game at Old Trafford and in the first half I had counted 54 passes that he made, 49 of which reached their target. With first-team opportunities limited with United, Darren and Sir Alex came to Molineux to discuss a transfer to Wolves. I well remember chatting to Sir Alex in my office while Graham talked to Darren. I mentioned to Sir Alex that I was aiming to watch Chelsea at Old Trafford in a few days' time as Wolves had been drawn against them in the FA Cup. He not only invited me to a pre-match meal, but while I was there gave me a photocopy of a dossier his staff had compiled on Chelsea. Wolves ultimately lost 1-0 to Chelsea, but this was a fine gesture on Sir Alex's part. Sir Alex also gave me his desk telephone number, which I used to good effect a few years later when seeking to fix up a pre-season friendly for Hereford United. That defeat at Chelsea was not in itself a disaster, but just two days later after staying down south Wolves lost 3-0 at Portsmouth in a League match. It appears that chairman Jonathan Hayward ordered the whole Wolves party back on the coach a few minutes after the end of the game. Graham Turner felt that his position was being undermined and resigned soon after arriving back in Wolverhampton. Peter Shirtliff was appointed caretaker manager and he and I had several chats, but a few days later Graham Taylor, whose previous job had been that of England manager, was appointed manager of Wolves. He asked me which players Wolves were currently watching and I mentioned, among others, a Motherwell forward Philip O'Donnell and Port Vale midfielder Ian Taylor. He said that he had a Scottish scout who would report on O'Donnell, but that he would like to accompany

me on a scouting mission to see Taylor. This we did and had a pleasant
evening, and he said that he could understand why I had been impressed
by this player. A few weeks later, however, I was asked by Graham Taylor
to meet him on the following Monday morning for coffee in his office.
He told me that he had only just realised my age and that he was about
to dispense with the position of chief scout and appoint an assistant manager with responsibility for scouting. I was not the only person to leave
Molineux at that time, as seventeen players were put on the transfer list.
The decks were being cleared for a new era.

Another chapter in my life had ended. I had had a wonderful time at
Molineux over the previous eight years. I felt that I had contributed to the
dramatic recovery of a team that I had first followed as a boy half a century
earlier. Promotion had been won in two successive seasons. A Wembley
final had been won. Gates had increased dramatically. I had enjoyed working with kindred spirits at a club for which I had a lifetime's affection. I
shall never cease to wonder whether in due course my partnership with
Graham Turner could have helped Wolves back to the top division. We
shall never know.

EIGHT

# BACK TO DERBY AND ON TO HEREFORD VIA BOLTON

*If a player has a bad game he is not necessarily a bad player.*

*Empty vessels make the most noise.*

After leaving Wolves in the summer of 1994 I received a phone call from Roy McFarland, asking if I would like to link up with him again at Derby. I was to work alongside Alan Durban, who was officially chief scout at the time but whose sphere of responsibility would not overlap with mine, as Roy was quick to reassure me. Alan would be mainly concerned with coaching activities and would travel with the first team.

Much had changed at the Baseball Ground since my previous spell there. Arthur Cox had moved on and some of the scouts had departed. Ken Guttridge was back there, however, while Billy McEwan was still looking after the reserves, for whom players such as Graham Harbey and David Linighan were making their mark. There were also some useful young players whom I remembered from my previous spell there, such as Scott Green and Craig Ramage. Right from the start, however, I knew that this second spell at Derby would almost certainly be a short one. Roy McFarland had been told that his contract would not be renewed beyond the end of that season. It was not the ideal situation for a chief scout as money was short and it seemed likely that more players would be sold than bought. Departures in that 1994/95 season included defender

Gary Charles to Aston Villa and striker Paul Kitson to Newcastle, both to ease the financial situation. One major signing during my relatively short spell back at Derby was midfielder Paul Trollope from Torquay. He was good value for the £100,000 fee and went on to win 4 full Welsh caps. After three seasons at Derby he went on to have five seasons at Fulham and shorter spells at Coventry and Northampton. He is at the time of writing with Bristol Rovers. I valued my contact with Torquay. Apart from Paul Trollope I signed defender Scott Stamps on trial but he was injured in his first game and returned to Torquay. I have the greatest respect for long-serving Torquay chairman Mike Bateson and I felt that both clubs benefited from the Trollope deal. Not only did he have three good seasons at Derby but he was sold on for £650,000 – a very useful profit.

Derby had a reasonable season in Division One, finishing in ninth spot with Marco Gabbiadini top scoring with 13 goals and midfielders Mark Pembridge and Paul Simpson getting 9 each. Before the end of the season, rumours that Roy McFarland's contract was not to be renewed became a reality and there were strong hints that his successor was to be Brian Horton. On the day the press conference was called, however, to introduce the new manager, it was Jim Smith who appeared. Initially Jim announced that there would be no immediate changes in the backroom staff. He intimated that he would talk with Gerry Summers and I the following day. We waited about for most of the day and then Jim can-celled the appointment because he was discussing a project with Edwina Currie, who was then MP for Derby. I therefore went home, only to be telephoned by Jim at teatime with the news that despite what he had said earlier he was going to bring in his own scouts. In fact Bobby Roberts, who had worked with him at Colchester was to be chief scout. I was to meet chairman Stuart Webb the following day to tie up loose ends. When I arrived at Stuart's office he was his usual efficient self, inviting me to lunch, settling up my contract, allowing me to keep my club car and also the 'float' in my expenses. Everything was settled quickly and properly.

Roy McFarland meanwhile had moved on to Bolton where he was to work as joint manager with Colin Todd, and he invited me to join him again. Bolton had just gained promotion to the Premier League. This job was going to be on just a temporary basis and it was in fact the first time I had worked outside the Midlands. I did manage, during my first few weeks, to sign Stuart Whitehead from Bromsgrove and he went on to have a useful career with Bolton, Carlisle and Darlington before rejoining me at Telford in 2003. I also recall persuading Ian McNeil, who was then Bolton chief scout, to come down to Moor Green to see James Smith (not the player of that name who went from Wolves to Crystal Palace) who had previously been with me at Wolves, but nothing materialised from this.

By this time Graham Turner had taken over as manager of Hereford in succession to Greg Downs and John Layton, and he invited me to join him and bring to the club, as he put it, some football expertise and a friendly face as he sought to improve the fortunes of a club that had ended up in sixteenth place in Division Three in 1994/95. It was agreed that I should work from home so that there would not be the excessive daily travelling of my Derby County days. It also meant that I was renewing a partnership with Graham Turner, with whom I had worked successfully at both Shrewsbury and Wolves, and I looked forward to this third spell with a man for whom I had the highest regard and respect. Hereford were then in their twenty-third season as a Football League club and my memories of them went back to my own playing days when they had teams in the Southern League and the Birmingham League. They had won the hearts of fans up and down the country when beating Newcastle United in the memorable FA Cup replay in 1972 when Colin Addison was in charge. Later that year they had gained election to the Fourth Division of the Football League in place of Barrow and had gone on to win promotion to the Third Division after just one season. They had even spent one season in the old Second Division under John Sillett in 1976/77. They were now in their eighteenth successive season in the Fourth Division that had by now changed its label to Division Three. They had got off to a good start with a 4-1 win over Barnet, with goalkeeper Chris MacKenzie scoring one of the goals with a long clearance from his own half that deceived young Barnet 'keeper Maik Taylor who, at the time of writing, is playing regularly for Birmingham in the Premiership.

Players already there when I arrived included former Walsall defender Dean Smith, former Leicester defender Tony James, much-travelled former Swindon striker Steve White and Tim Steele, whom I had signed for Shrewsbury in 1985 and for Wolves in 1989. My first involvement in a signing for Hereford was that of busy blond teenage midfielder

Jamie Pitman, who was on the 'open to offers' list at Swindon and whom I had seen playing for Scarborough reserves at Walsall while he was on trial at the Yorkshire club. I contacted Swindon youth-team coach John Trollope (whose son Paul I had signed for Derby from Torquay some years earlier) for information about Jamie and finally signed him in February 1996. He played in a total of 13 games before the end of that season, including the two play-off semi-finals against Darlington less than a month after dislocating a shoulder at Mansfield. Others signed during that first season at Hereford included Keith Downing, who had been with Graham and I both at Shrewsbury and at Wolves, striker Chris Hargreaves, whom I had seen on many occasions scoring goals for West Bromwich Albion reserves, and former Wolverhampton schoolboy Darren Evans on a free transfer from Aston Villa, whom he had joined straight from school. Another Wolverhampton-born player whom I was pleased to sign was central defender Stuart Watkiss, who had had a brief spell with Wolves early in his career and had done well for Walsall in the early 1990s. Then there was central defender Steve Blatherwick, who had 10 games on loan from Nottingham Forest before moving on to Chesterfield. It is worth noting that all these signings came from the Midlands area. Graham and I always felt that this gave us a better chance of knowing what we were getting. Geographical location is very important when recruiting players.

Overall this had been an interesting first season at Hereford. A highlight had been the third round FA Cup tie against Spurs, which ended 1-1 at Edgar Street in front of an 8,806 gate before losing the replay 5-1 at White Hart Lane. Though the semi-final of the play-offs ended in a 4-2 aggregate defeat by Darlington, this was a vast improvement on the sixteenth place of the previous season.

As we prepared for the 1996/97 season several new singings were made. In general, players with a Midland connection were sought as this would facilitate travelling and avoid the difficulties and expense of relocation. Striker Gavin Mahon, whom I had taken to Wolves from Kings Norton Schools and who had now been released, was signed and two years later moved on to Brentford for a substantial fee. He later moved on to Watford, for whom he was voted Player of the Season in 2003/04. Adrian Foster, who was well known to me from his West Bromwich Albion days was signed from Gillingham, where he had been leading scorer with 18 goals including a hat-trick in a 3-2 win at Carlisle in March. David Norton, who numbered Aston Villa among his former clubs, was brought into the defence and also helped with coaching, while Nicky Law also figured in the defence, albeit for just a short spell. Hereford was his ninth Football League club and in the eleven games he played he showed that he was still possessed of a fierce tackle and an extremely long throw. He has since managed Chesterfield and Bradford City. Midfielders Micky Forsyth (whom I had known at Derby) and Gavin O'Toole were taken on loan from Notts County and Coventry respectively, but injury forced Gavin out after just one game. Goalkeeper Andy De Bont, who had joined Wolves straight from school, was well-known to Graham and I and played for the first half of the season but was then succeeded by former Port Vale and Walsall man Trevor Wood. Carl Beeston, whom I had been close to signing for Wolves from Stoke, came on loan and played a few games in midfield early in the season while John Williams, a Birmingham-born and much-travelled striker, came from Wycombe in February and played a few games up front with limited success.

Results were not going well and a further influx of signings took place near transfer deadline day. Brian McGorry from Wycombe, Bradley Sandeman from Northampton and Graham Turner's son Mark from Telford all came into midfield. Mark had played just one game for Wolves in 1992 when his father was manager there, and I felt that he suffered as a result of being the manager's son as Graham made particularly high demands on him. He has been with Tamworth in more recent times and I felt that this good honest professional (like his father before him) deserved to go further in the game. A total of 34 players were used in that 1996/97 season and I felt that the club suffered from seeming to many people to be off the map. Time and again I was asked by prospective players where Hereford was, as if they regarded it as one of the outposts of civilisation.

Hereford also suffered from having only a limited number of reserve games. One of my big regrets during my time there was that not much progress was made with the younger element of schoolboy and youth football. This was largely because of the financial aspect and the situation was exacerbated when Hereford lost their School of Excellence when losing their Football League status. At one stage Hereford 'adopted' North Birmingham College and (erroneously in my view) labelled them the

'Hereford youth eleven'. This venture did not produce one first-team player. Financially and geographically Hereford were certainly at a disadvantage when it came to youth football.

My second season at Hereford reached an unhappy climax on 3 May 1997 when they needed to win the final game at home against Brighton in order to retain their Football League status. A crowd of 8,532 packed into Edgar Street (just under 300 fewer than for the Spurs FA Cup tie in the previous season) but, although Hereford dominated the first half, the final score was 1-1. Thus it was Conference football for Hereford in 1997/98. Graham Turner offered his resignation but this was not accepted and he resolved that, as he was the manager who took them out of the Football League, he should be the one to take them back. This was very commendable and very well received. In the course of 1997/98 Graham took over as chairman from Peter Hill and asked me to join the board. This I reluctantly agreed to do, as I am never happy about employees being board members. A local journalist wrote that the way back would not be easy, but that the attempt to achieve it would be character building. How right he was.

Now the challenge was for me to help to get together a team that would make its mark in the Conference. This was a new experience for me, but I found myself looking in the same places for players that I had explored in Hereford's Football League days. Graham and I both thought that this would be the right policy. New signings included Neil Grayson, a striker who had not played in the Football League until he joined Doncaster at the age of twenty-five, and had recently been with Northampton. Ian Rodgerson, who had been with Hereford from 1985 to 1988 and had since had two spells with Cardiff and one each with Birmingham and Sunderland, returned to strengthen the defence, where another new signing, Richard Walker from Notts County, added to the options, being a left-sided player also able to operate as a left-sided central defender. Graham and I had both seen him in the Notts County reserve side and he proved to be particularly strong as a central defender. It was in this role that he was in due course sold to Cheltenham. All three new signings played in the opening game against Welling. This was lost 2-1, but the gate of 3,138, while less than half the number who had watched the final Football League game against Brighton, was just over 100 more than the previous season's average.

Loan players in 1997/98 included goalkeeper Mark Gayle, formerly with Walsall and Worcester, midfielder Andy Milner from Chester and striker Richard Leadbeater, who had been at Molineux during my time there, first in the School of Excellence and then on a YTS. A final position of seventh in this first Conference season was 20 points behind Conference winners Halifax Town, but the season was brightened by a first round FA Cup win over Brighton, which provided some slight consolation for the fateful draw against them six months earlier. Gates, which had slipped below the 2,000 mark in February, were back above 3,000 in the last few weeks of the season and all in all I felt that there was something to build on for the following season at this brave little club where, inevitably, everything was on a much smaller scale than I had experienced at my previous three clubs, Derby, Wolves and Bolton.

It was during the summer of 1998 that I made one of my best-ever non-League signings for Hereford in the person of midfielder John Snape from Halesowen. John had been a junior with West Bromwich Albion and had gained a wealth of experience with Bromsgrove, Northfield, Stourbridge and Halesowen. He was a born leader whose professional attitude set a fine example to all around him, full-time and part-time. Andy Quy, a former Derby junior, had come from Kettering in the course of the previous season and missed only three games in goal, and we were fortunate in having cover for this vital position in Mark Jones, an elder brother of Paul Jones of Wolves and Southampton fame. Mark was a part-timer who worked on the family farm in Wem and made national headlines in December 2000 when playing the games of his life in the third round FA Cup tie against Leicester City, when Hereford went down to an extra-time goal from Muzzy Izzet in the replay.

In that 1998/99 season Ian Wright missed only five games at the heart of the defence. He had been signed in the summer of 1998 from Hull after I had seen him in a reserve game at Walsall. He went on to become Hereford club captain. Mark Taylor, an experienced midfielder, also missed just five games. I remembered signing Mark for Shrewsbury Town from Newton Albion as a teenager while I was at the Gay Meadow with Graham and he had had a successful career with Walsall and Sheffield Wednesday in the meantime. Another well-known name who played a few games near the end of 1998/99 was former Wolves midfielder Robbie Dennison who, eleven years earlier, had scored a spectacular goal in the Sherpa Van Trophy final against Burnley at Wembley. Even so, 1998/99 was rather a disappointing season with a final position of thirteenth and little progress in cup competitions.

One bright spot towards the end of that season, however, was the emergence of Paul Parry from the junior ranks. He showed up well on the left flank and made steady progress over the next few seasons. Hereford fans still talk about his shot in the FA Cup tie against Leicester that came back off a post when it could well have been the match-winner. Paul was eventually to join Cardiff in January 2004 and a few months later got the match-winner for Wales in a friendly game against Canada. I had repeatedly asked scouting friends of mine with senior clubs to come and watch Paul, as I thought that he was capable of making the grade on a bigger stage. I was surprised that it took so long for his talents to be recognised by bigger clubs. I felt that they were very remiss.

Season 1999/00 was rather happier, with a final position of eighth in the Conference and a young, developing side that included Rob Elmes, a teacher who had first attracted attention while playing for Halesowen at a time when I was watching John Snape a couple of seasons earlier. He had done well in a side inspired by former Aston Villa and Wolves midfielder Paul Birch. Rob scored twice in his first full game for Hereford against Kettering in August 1999 and went on to get 15 goals in that first season with Hereford. One of Rob's goals proved to be the match-winner against Hartlepool that earned the third round FA Cup tie with Leicester already referred to. The brave displays against Leicester seemed to breathe new life into the whole club and they were followed by an unbeaten run of 11 games.

One newcomer in the second half of the season was experienced goalkeeper Scott Cooksey, who took over from Mark Jones soon after the latter's heroic displays against Leicester. Scott had had Football League experience with Peterborough and Shrewsbury and it was unfortunate that, after a good season and a half with Hereford he had to retire through injury at the age of twenty-nine in 2001. He then showed resourcefulness in studying for a Sports Studies degree before entering the teaching profession at a school in Aldridge.

The summer of 2000 saw Hereford looking for an experienced player-coach to succeed Keith Downing, who had returned to Wolves in join their coaching staff. Two more former Wolves players were approached, namely Kevin Keen and Phil Robinson. Kevin eventually moved to Macclesfield, as he felt that he was capable of at least one more season in the Football League. Phil was therefore signed as player-coach and figured in the Hereford team that reached the semi-final of the FA Trophy. Hereford seemed all set for the final when they drew at Forest Green in the semi-final. Forest Green, however, played out of their skins to win the second leg 4-1 and a dream ending to Hereford's season failed to materialise.

Another former Wolves man, Steve Bull, also floated briefly across the Hereford scene in 2000/01. Having been forced out of League football by injury he had acquired coaching badges and was eager to get back into the game in some capacity, though he lacked coaching experience. He was invited by Graham Turner to join Hereford's pre-season training and in the course of the season he made 7 substitute appearances and scored late equalisers against Nuneaton in February and against Morecambe in April. Steve was at that time also working for Wolves, receiving sponsors on match days.

My most exciting signing in this 2000/01 season was midfielder Mike McIndoe, whom I had seen playing for Luton reserves the previous season. When his agent Lorraine Gates informed me that he was available, Graham and I moved quickly to meet him and he was signed in time to play in the opening game of the season against Southport. He had an excellent left foot and missed only one game until moving to Yeovil in February 2001. He moved on to Doncaster where he was voted Player of the Season in 2003/04 and won a Scottish 'B' international cap. When Mike moved from Yeovil he was replaced by another ex-Hereford man, namely Gavin Williams, who steadily progressed from the junior ranks, making his debut as an eighteen-year-old in 1998 and progressing steadily until moving to Yeovil in 2002 and winning a Player of the Year award in their first Football League season of 2003/04. My feelings with regard to Gavin were exactly the same as with Paul Parry, namely that bigger clubs were slow to recognise his potential. He had helped Hereford to a good start in 2001/02 when he had got the winner in the televised opening

Colin Taylor. My first and one of my greatest ever signings. He tallied a total of 189 goals in 502 games in three spells with Walsall.

*This page*: Bill Moore (*above left*) and Ray Shaw (*above right*). Two managers of contrasting character who both helped me tremendously in my first spell at Walsall.

*Opposite page*: Nick Atthey (*top left*), Stan Bennett (*top right*), Frank Gregg (*bottom left*) and Colin Harrison (*bottom right*). Four Walsall discoveries of the 1960s who were all one-club men and who played a combines total of 1,914 games.

Allan Clarke (*left*) and George Kirby (*right*). The perfect example of youth and experience combining as twin strikers.

Ken Hill (*left*) and Brian Caswell (*right*). I taught them at day school and when I was chief scout at Walsall I found them to be salt-of-the-earth professionals.

*Opposite page*:
Four excellent
goalkeepers, Alan
Boswell (*top
left*), Phil Parkes
(*top right*) and
Mark Wallington
(*bottom left*),
joined Walsall
during my first
spell there and
Ron Green (*bottom right*)
signed during my second
spell.

*This page:* Ernie Thomas
(Walsall, *top left*), Ken
Wheldon (Walsall, *top
right*) and Tim Yates
(Shrewsbury, *right*) were
chairmen of contrasting
character who did great
work for their respective
clubs.

*Opposite page*: Kenny Mower (*top left*), Craig Shakespeare (*top right*), David Preece (*bottom left*) and Mark Rees (*bottom right*). Four of my signings as Walsall juniors who all went on to play in the Milk Cup semi-final team of 1984.

*This page*: Nigel Pearson (*below, second row, second from left*), Colin Robinson (*below, second row, third from left*), Tim Steele (*below, front row, extreme left*) and Gary Hackett (*right*). Four Shrewsbury signings who all went on to 'bigger' clubs.

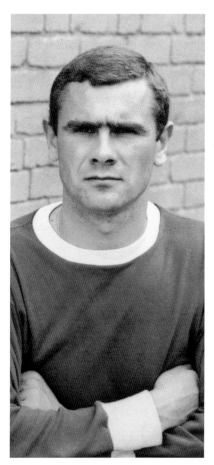 

*This page*: Arthur Cox (*above left*) and Roy McFarland (*above right*), manager and assistant manager when I joined Derby and who regarded first team and reserve team as equally important.

*Opposite page*: Phil Gee (*top left*), Martin Taylor (*top right*), Paul Trollope (*bottom left*) and David Penney (*bottom right*). Four players whom I signed for Derby and who have in different ways fully justified their early promise.

Graham Turner (*above left*). How lucky I was to work with Graham at three different clubs.

Steve Bull (*above right*), Andy Thompson (*left*), Robbie Dennison (*opposite above*) and Mark Venus (*opposite below*), all of whom, after early experience with other clubs, fulfilled themselves at Wolves and lifted the club from lower Fourth Division to upper Second Division.

*Anti-clockwise from top*: Jamie Pitman, Gavin Mahon, Mike McIndoe and Robert Purdie. Jamie was my first Hereford signing and has had two successful spells with them. Gavin and Mike moved on to successful League careers and Robert is now one of the outstanding players in the Conference.

# HEREFORD UNITED F.C. (1939) LTD

*Registered Office:*
Edgar Street Athletic Ground
Hereford HR4 9JU
Telephone: (01432) 276666
Fax: (01432) 341359
Bulls Bulletin: (0891) 555808
VAT No: 133 7291 75
Registered in England No: 355272

TRIALISTS.

MIDLAND CONFERENCE.

Hereford Limited v. Stoke City - Wed. 31st March, 99.

| | | | | | |
|---|---|---|---|---|---|
| O/N. | Fraser Sidebottom. 24/12/80 | R.B. | Barnsley. | ▰▰▰▰▰▰ | Barnsley. |
| O/N. | Martin Eldridge. 27/11/80 | L.B. | Norwich | ▰▰▰▰▰▰ | Holbeach |
| | James Wall. 21/3/80 | C.H. | Derby Co. | ▰▰▰▰▰▰ | Derby |
| O/N. | Robert Smith. 4/11/80 | C.H. | Norwich. | ▰▰▰▰▰▰ | Milton Keynes |
| O/N. | Ian Richards. 5/10/79. | M.F. | Blackburn. | ▰▰▰▰▰▰ | Barnsley. |
| | Craig Hanson. 15/12/80 | Striker | Derby Co. | ▰▰▰▰▰▰ | Derby. |
| O/N. | David Moray. 18/3/81 | CH | Norwich. | ▰▰▰▰▰▰ | East London. |
| | James Hince. | M.F. | West B.A. | ▰▰▰▰▰▰ | Birmingham |
| | Barrington Belgrave 16/9/80 | Striker | Norwich | ▰▰▰▰▰▰ | London. |
| | Shaun Carr. 15/12/80. | Striker | Norwich. | ▰▰▰▰▰▰ | London. |

**Sun Valley**
*Club Sponsor*

O/N = Overnight Stay.

DIRECTORS: Mr P.S. Hill F.R.I.C.S.(Chairman), Mr R.A. Fry (Managing Direcor)
Mr D.H. Vaughan (Secretary), Mr J. Duggan (Financial Director)
Ms J. Simmons (Commercial Director)

A sample of the paperwork for a trial game arranged for young players in whom a club is interested.

Chris Murphy (*above*), Stuart Whitehead (*right*), Lee Mills (*below left*) and Gary Stanley (*below right*) were four players I signed for Telford before their well-documented financial problems which the club did well to survive.

game against Barnet, who had just lost their Football League place. Hopes were then high that Hereford would improve on their eleventh spot of the previous season, particularly when they lost only 1 of their first 7 games. Sadly, however, there were few bright spots after that, one of them being the FA Cup win over Wrexham in November with skipper Ian Wright getting the winner, followed by a narrow 3-2 defeat at Swindon in the second round. Young left-flank defender Tony Capaldi played in both those thrilling FA Cup games while on loan from Birmingham City, and I would have been happy to sign him on a more permanent basis. At the end of the season he was snapped up by Plymouth Argyle and is, at the time of writing, holding his own with them in the Championship. The biggest disappointment to me during the season was that we were unable to field our strongest side for several weeks owing to injuries. Two senior players missed most of the first half of the season after operations, and this was particularly disheartening. A final position of seventeenth in 2001/02 was disappointing, but the board still felt that Graham was the man to motivate the team, though the dreaded vote of confidence was not given. Phil Robinson's contract was not renewed and he moved to Stafford Rangers as manager. Thoughts therefore turned towards the appointment of a new Hereford coach and in due course Richard O'Kelly, who had recently parted company with West Bromwich Albion, took over. I had signed Richard as a player for Walsall from Alvechurch in 1979 and his intelligent approach to the game as a player had carried over into his coaching. He was working for the Post Office after leaving West Bromwich Albion and had been talking to Rushden & Diamonds regarding a position there when I approached him and persuaded him to send his CV to Hereford. Initially, his position as coach was combined with that of physiotherapist, and his bubbly personality made an immediate impact on the dressing room.

Richard's first season at Hereford in 2002/03 coincided with a rise of eleven places to sixth in the Conference. It was a delight for me to see the success of Robert Purdie, for whom Graham and I had negotiated during the summer of 2002. Robert had been mentioned by Leicester coach Alan Hill when I had asked who was being released from their School of Excellence. Robert came with two other lads to play in a practice match at Hereford and Alan said at the time that he might live to regret releasing him. Graham and I were immediately impressed by his skills in the practice game and by the way he conducted himself in the subsequent interview at junction ten of the M6. Terms could not be agreed initially but after Robert had been unimpressed on a subsequent visit to Lincoln City we had a second meeting with him. At this meeting a slight increase was made to the terms offered and to my delight Robert signed. In his first two seasons at Hereford he has done well, playing mainly up front, but I am not sure which position will ultimately turn out to be his best, as he is a fine all-round player whom I feel will make his mark in the game.

Another good all-rounder who emerged in 2002/03 was Danny Williams, who impressed on the right side of midfield. I had liked the look of him when he was playing for Chesterfield reserves and his enthusiasm carried over after his move to Hereford. His particular delight was in taking free-kicks. I was also pleased to sign defender Andy Tretton, whom I had known since his days in the Derby County youth team and who had just been released by Shrewsbury Town.

Two strikers who had their moments in 2002/03 were Steve Guinan and John Grant. Steve numbered Nottingham Forest, Darlington, Burnley, Halifax, Cambridge, Crewe, Plymouth and Shrewsbury among his former clubs and, though he had not built up a great goalscoring record, he was well-built and a good leader of the front line. He had a good first season at Edgar Street in 2002/03, his 14 goals including a hat-trick against Barnet in November. I had seen John at Northwich in the previous season and, though he had some off-field problems, he played regularly in the second half of the season without becoming a regular scorer. He followed in the footsteps of two former Wolves juniors, Steve Piearce and Scott Voice, who both had spells at Hereford but did not score the regular goals that they had done in their earlier days.

We had high hopes of Robert Sawyers, a left-flank attacker who had been released by Wolves and had then gone to Barnet after we had tried to sign him. He was not happy down south and we signed him in the summer of 2002, but by then he had lost his edge and after the first few weeks of the season played only the occasional game. This was very disappointing. Goalkeeper Matt Baker, whom I had originally seen playing in the Pontins League for Hull City, was ever-present in 2002/03 while defender Michael Rose missed only one game. He was one of two brothers in the Manchester United junior ranks and we met him and his father at junction ten of the M6. Though he was reluctant at first to move out of the Football League, we pointed out that joining Hereford could well be the way back there and, after signing for Hereford, he quickly settled down as a reliable defender. Indeed he became probably the best left-footed player in the Conference. Yeovil must have thought so as they signed him during the following close season.

Thus, despite financial problems, Hereford finished sixth in 2002/03 and seemed to have the potential to challenge for promotion in the following season. I felt, however, that the time had come for me to leave. I attended a board meeting in which it was clear that the financial situation was no better than it had been for some time. It had been difficult to work in such an economic climate. I saw no light at the end of the financial tunnel. I arranged a meeting with Graham a few days after the last game of the season. I handed him my letter of resignation. He asked me to reconsider and commented that it would be the end of an era. Tears were shed on both sides. There was no falling out. It was pure economics that caused me to leave. This was the right time for me to go if there ever could be a right time. I left with the greatest admiration for Graham and for secretary Joan Fennessy, who had jointly carried the responsibility of running the club. Graham is a tremendous motivator of players and I had every confidence that he would ultimately achieve success with his present group of players. He managed the club down to the last detail, even having a chef on the team coach to away games. Joan, meanwhile, had done virtually every job at the club, from drawing up contracts to polishing the boardroom table. I felt I was leaving behind not only friends but players who would do well for Hereford in the future. As I drove home I reflected on the agony of relegation from the Football League in 1997 and the ecstasy of those two great games against Leicester in the FA Cup in December 2000. I had worked with Graham for the best part of twenty years. He had sought my advice. He had trusted my judgement and had usually acted upon it. When seeking players we had a modus operandi that seemed to work – drawing up players from PFA lists that appeared in the summer, then checking on their playing records and their attitudes from people who knew them. Then, after whittling down the lists, we had interviewed them, taken careful note of their personalities and then those suitable we either invited for trials or in some cases tried to sign them straight away. We made every player aware that their main criterion in choosing whether to sign for a club should be not the stadium, not the money, but the people they would be working with. Graham and I also adhered to the maxim that whenever we had doubts about a player the answer was no.

As I left the Hereford car park, despite the overhanging financial cloud, I felt nothing but respect for the tremendous efforts of both Graham Turner and Joan Fennessy to revive Hereford's fortunes. My stomach was churning. I felt I was leaving behind players who would serve Hereford well in the future. Subsequent events have proved this to be quite correct. After a tremendous run at the end of 2003/04 they were narrowly pipped by Chester for automatic promotion. Though they beat Chester in the final League game of the season this of course counted for nothing as they went out on penalties to Aldershot in the semi-final of the play-offs after having Andy Tretton sent off in the first half.

I still have nothing but admiration for Graham Turner who, since relegation to the Conference in 1997, has served them jointly as chairman and manager. Such a joint role is virtually impossible to fulfil and I'm sure Graham would agree that chairmanship is not his forte. His managerial acumen, however, has taken them to within an ace of a return to the Football League, where he vowed he would take them when his resignation was turned down by the board in 1997. He has done all this with very little financial underpinning. Graham's management has been an object lesson for all managers of smaller clubs. I'm sure that he could show many the way to run a Football League club, though his chances of getting there are now limited by being owner and chairman as well as manager of Hereford. Graham is a great football man with his particular strength that of motivating players. It was a privilege to work alongside him at three different clubs. I sincerely hope that Hereford's return to the Football League is just around the corner.

As this book was being completed I was interested to read in the September issue of the *Non-League Newspaper* the dream team chosen by Tony James, the present Hereford captain in whose signing from West Bromwich Albion I had been involved during my time at Edgar Street. It read: Terry Roberts (Dagenham) in goal; Andy Tretton (Hereford),

Ian Wright (Burton and ex-Hereford) and Terry Skiverton (Yeovil) in the back line; Gavin Williams (Yeovil and ex-Hereford) Gavin Mahon (Watford and ex-Hereford) and Mike McIndoe (Doncaster and ex-Hereford) in central midfield; Paul Parry (Cardiff and ex-Hereford) right midfield; Michael Rose (Yeovil and ex-Hereford) left midfield; and Darryl Clare (Chester) and Steve Guinan (Cheltenham and ex-Hereford) up front. While at Hereford I was closely connected with the signing of Tretton, Wright, Rose, Mahon, McIndoe and Guinan, while I also saw Williams and Parry develop during my time there. I must have been doing something right.

# NINE

# AND SO TO TELFORD UNITED

*If there's any doubt as to whether to sign a player or not, the answer is no.*

*If you want a job doing ask a busy man.*

O ver the years I had known Wellington Town as a friendly non-League
club, playing in the old Cheshire League before joining the Southern
League in 1958. They changed their name to Telford United in 1969 and
became founder members of the Football Conferencs in 1979. As a Conference
side they had earned something of a nationwide reputation for FA Cup giant-
killing, their victims including Bradford City, Darlington, Stockport, Stoke
and Wigan, and they had fully extended Everton in a fifth round tie in 1985.
They shared with Northwich Victoria the distinction of being the only side
to hold on to their Conference place for the first twenty-five years of its
existence and won the FA Trophy in 1972, 1983 and 1989. Their ground at
the Bucks Head on the A5 had been dramatically modernised in 2002 and
2003 and in visits both before and after the refurbishment I had found the
club to be extremely hospitable. Over the years I had visited the ground on
many occasions, encouraged not only by the excellent hospitality but by the
easy access by road via the A5 and then later via the M54. These visits had
enabled me to keep up not only with the Telford team, but also with more
distant visiting teams. Lots of ex-Football League players had found their way
to Wellington and Telford in the later stages of their careers, among them
Johnny Hancocks, a particular favourite of mine, Geoff Hurst, Ron Flowers,
Gordon Banks, Wayne Clarke and Andy Mutch, several of these having spells

as manager. In fact, they had had over the years quite a turnover of managers, but they had also fielded some splendidly consistent players, among
them goalkeeper Kevin Charlton, defender Chris McGinty, midfielder Eddie
Hogan, winger John Alcock and striker Jack Bentley, whose son Jim Bentley
later became almost as effective a defender as Jack had been a striker.

In recent years I had met Telford chairman Andy Shaw on a number of
occasions at Telford, at Hereford when his team had been visiting there and
at Hednesford, where he had formerly been a director. He really did seem
to be the epitome of enthusiasm and hard work, wanting to be involved in
every aspect of the club's development without interfering with those who
were doing a good job in their own particular sphere. Andy's enthusiasm
was inspirational. Within a short time of leaving Hereford in the summer
of 2003 I was very happy to be contacted by Mr Shaw and he invited me
to join Telford United and to work for them as chief scout alongside newly
appointed manager Mick Jones. Mick, like myself, had had a previous spell
with Derby though not at the same time. He had considerable experience
as a player with Notts County and Peterborough, as assistant manager and
coach to several lower division clubs and as manager of Peterborough,
Plymouth, Kettering (with whom he won the FA Trophy) and Halifax.
Since returning from Brunei, where he had been national coach, he had
been helping out at Nuneaton under manager Steve Burr, and therefore
had some recent knowledge of the Conference.

Soon I found myself at a press conference on a May Monday morning
in 2003 with Mick saying to the assembled scribes, 'I'm glad Ron's here.
It's good to be working with him.' Chairman Andy Shaw had said that he
wished to use my experience and at first wished to give me a high-sounding
title. I was not happy about this and, after much discussion, we settled for
'chief scout', the label I had worked under at Walsall, Shrewsbury, Derby,
Wolves and Hereford. He said that he wanted me to be adviser on all football
matters and, although I didn't really want a place on the board, he insisted
that I had one. Though, as I have said before, I have always felt that it isn't
in an individual's best interests to be both an employee and a director of a
club, there are times when there is no suitable alternative.

All of the playing staff of the previous season of 2002/03 had been released
with the exception of Paul Moore, a young ex-Wolves player who had scored
14 goals that season, and so we started the building of a new team with

virtually carte blanche. Soon I was sitting down with Mick Jones to compile a wanted list from the PFA list of players available and clubs' individual lists of players released. Mick had spent most of the previous three years abroad, so he was eager to catch up with comings and goings during that time. As asides to our main conversations, he constantly reminded me of the fact that, during my time at Wolves, his Halifax side had been something of a bogey team and had dismissed the danger of Steve Bull with impunity.

As Mick and I listed possible signings from the lists before us, we agreed to follow the tried and tested method I had used with Graham Turner at Hereford. A preliminary phone call would be made to a player to establish contact. When appropriate, a personal meeting would be arranged and, before meeting the player, we would check up on age and experience and look at any statistics that may be available. Then in the face-to-face meeting we would assess the player's enthusiasm and attitude to football and to life and find out his domestic circumstances. If the vibes were positive we would then move on to discussion of a possible contract.

In those May days of 2003, Andy, Mick and I met regularly and the *Non-League Newspaper* labelled us the 'Three Musketeers'. Interest in Telford United was running high in the town, sparked by advance publicity and helped by the fact that local rivals Shrewsbury Town had just been relegated from the Football League. This meant that they would be playing alongside Telford in the Conference and now at last Telford had a chance of becoming the most successful club in Shropshire. The pre-season open morning brought in more fans than ever before on such an occasion and in fact the number of people there exceeded the average attendance at Conference games the previous season.

The players on PFA lists were many and varied and from all divisions. Among them were a number that I had signed for previous clubs, or with whom I had had contact in previous seasons. Some were quickly signed, some were invited to play in pre-season games so that they could be seen in action – either in the home games arranged or on the pre-season tour of the West Country. As Telford were now a full-time club, chairman Andy Shaw obviously played a vital part in all contractual discussions. As we moved towards settling on a team with which to start the Conference season, there was little need for discussion about a number-one goalkeeper. I had seen Chris MacKenzie over the years in his days at Leyton Orient, Corby and Hereford, and Mick Jones had seen him recently at Nuneaton, where he had just had a very good season. The only delay in signing him was that Chris needed time to give up his outside job in order to become a full-time professional, and he also had to move home from the Loughborough area. We then looked for a second 'keeper, thinking initially of a young player with prospects. I then saw in the press, however, that Martin Taylor had just played his last game for Wycombe. Martin was one of a number of Football League players to graduate from Tamworth club Mile Oak and I had previously signed him for Derby where he had clocked up over 100 League and cup games up to 1996. Since then he had played over 250 games for Wycombe. While at Derby he had suffered a serious injury, seen by millions on television, requiring surgery, but had recovered well enough to be voted Player of the Season at Wycombe for more than one campaign. I knew that Martin lived on the Burton side of Derby and I persuaded him to meet Andy, Mick and myself at the Spread Eagle on the A5. After lengthy discussion he agreed to become our goalkeeping coach and to be ready to play in emergency as he was still only thirty-six, an age at which many goalkeepers are still at or near their best. This arrangement fitted in with his work for a building company that he had set up and to which he was planning to devote all his energies after retiring from football. We were pleased to get him.

With regard to defenders I knew of Neil Howarth, who had seen service with Kidderminster, Cheltenham and Macclesfield and had captained both the latter clubs. I contacted Graham Allner, whom I had signed as a teenager for Walsall and who had in more recent times managed both Kidderminster and Cheltenham. He gave me positive vibes with regard to Neil and the signing was quickly made. Stuart Whitehead was another player I was pleased to add to the Telford defensive strength. I had signed him as a teenager from Bromsgrove Rovers during my brief spell at Bolton. Though he did not make the Bolton first team he was a regular reserve and then moved on via Carlisle to Darlington, playing in nearly 200 games for these two northern clubs. He was now keen to return to the Midlands. I felt that the relationship that I had built up with Stuart and his family some years before when signing him as a teenager for Bolton had helped to clinch the move to Telford. Players are in general reluctant to move out of the Football League to a non-League club and Stuart took some time to make up his mind. He was ultimately glad to come nearer his roots, particularly as his future wife succeeded in getting a job as receptionist in the hotel at the Bucks Head.

Another player whom we managed to sign after some initial hesitation was Scott Green. Scott was a native of Darlaston, near Walsall, whom I had signed for Derby from Walsall Pegasus (a Walsall under-18 side) way back in the 1980s. Pegasus were a side managed by Bob Thomas, over the years producing a number of players who had moved into the Football League. After a spell in Scandinavia he had moved to Bolton in 1990 and played over 200 games for them before moving to Wigan in 1997 for a reported £200,000. He then played over 200 games for Wigan and it was at one of the last of these that I met up with him again when he was playing in an LDV Vans Trophy match at Hereford in 2002. While chatting with him before the game I had joked with him about scoring the winner, and he did just that in the last minute of the game. Scott was equally happy in defence and midfield and 2002/03 had seen him playing in the same Wrexham side as Darren Ferguson and Northern Ireland 'B' player Jeff Whitley. When I saw he was on the available list in the summer of 2003 I invited him over for talks. Mick Jones, Andy Shaw and I met him at the Bowling Green, Lichfield, and for two hours Mick talked football with him and Andy talked finance, and the outcome was a two-year contract that he signed next day after talking it over with his wife. We also tried unsuccessfully to sign Jeff Whitley around this time.

When the question of first-team coach arose, the name of Davie Preece came readily to mind. I had signed this busy little midfielder (who hailed from the Bridgnorth area) in my Walsall days and he had gone on to have a fine career with Luton and a number of other clubs. More recently he had been Roy McFarland's assistant at Cambridge and Torquay. I knew David well and, on talking to him, found that he would be very pleased to move back nearer to his Bridgnorth home. Mick had also known him for some time and was happy to take him on.

As usual I was looking for left-sided players both for defence and attack, and two who impressed in a pre-season game against Sheffield United were Trevor Challis and Fitzroy Simpson, who had been released by Bristol Rovers and Walsall respectively. In this win over Sheffield United Telford had begun to look like a team and, after the game, Andy, Mick and I met with the two players and their agents in the boardroom and a deal was done with both players. Trevor was destined to start the season on the left side of the defence with Matt Clarke on the right. Matt was a Black Country lad and I had taken him to Wolves on a YTS. After being released by Wolves he played for Halesowen and Kidderminster before I signed him again, this time for Hereford. When Hereford released him Andy Shaw moved in quickly to take him to Telford.

Inevitably we took on far more trialists than we actually retained. Two midfielders who came from Cambridge on the recommendation of our new coach David Preece were Scott Eustace and Neil Mustoe. Scott was kept long enough to play 5 first-team games at the start of the season, but Neil was released after pre-season. A more permanent midfield signing was Richard Lavery from Nuneaton. Mick Jones had known him while helping out at Nuneaton in 2002/03 and, while he was a splendidly competitive player, there was always the danger that he would be a victim of his own over-enthusiasm. Another player with Nuneaton connections was Sam Ricketts, who had had a spell on loan there while with Oxford. I had tried to sign Sam for Hereford in his Oxford days but he had declined. Now, after four years with Oxford in which he had played just 48 games, he was ready for a move. Sam had just recovered from a broken collarbone and he had an interesting sporting pedigree, being the son of show jumper Derek Ricketts and a nephew of former jockey Johnny Francombe. Sam soon proved himself to be a really versatile player with two good feet, scoring in his opening game against Gravesend in August and gaining representative honours for the England non-League side later in the season.

Meanwhile, a player who scored on his home debut for Telford (against Exeter) was Lee Mills, another player whose previous links with me helped considerably in his signing. I had signed him for Wolves from Stocksbridge in 1992 as recounted in a previous chapter and, in a career embracing eight different League clubs, he had scored over 100 league and cup goals at the rate of one every three games. I knew he was living at Brocton between Penkridge and Stafford, having married a Penkridge girl in his Wolves days, and he readily agreed to have discussions. These took place at Acton Trussell just outside Stafford. During our conversation there he said that he'd like to see the new ground at Telford. This was agreed for the next day and he was impressed enough to telephone his agent and set up further discussions. These led to him signing for Telford and, in due course, scoring the winning goal in an FA Cup tie at Crewe. While we were negotiating with Lee we also attempted to sign Marvin Robinson, a former Wolverhampton Grammar School boy whose mother was a nurse in Wolverhampton. He had scored goals for both Stoke and Tranmere while on loan to them in 2002/03, but he declined the Telford offer and departed for the United States before the season began.

Another striker I should like to have paired up with Lee Mills was Marc Richards, who hailed from Rugeley and had moved from Hednesford to Blackburn (a fee being involved) in 1999 where he linked up with former Wolves man Robert Kelly, who was youth coach there. In recent years he had scored a decisive penalty for Blackburn against Walsall in a Worthington Cup game and had had loan spells at Crewe, Oldham, Halifax and Swansea, scoring 7 goals in 17 games for the Swans. I really fancied his lethal right foot scoring goals for Telford and had talked to him and his family at length. At the age of twenty-one, however, he wanted to stay in League football and he moved to Northampton and scored 11 goals in 2003/04. I was, however, grateful to Jim Waddell, a car salesman in Lichfield with whom I have done business over the years for putting me in touch with the Richards family, as he lived in the same street as them in Rugeley.

'Some you win, some you lose' is a maxim that every scout has to accept. We initially took on trial at Telford Lee Williams, who had seen service with Aston Villa and Peterborough and had just been released by Cheltenham. He did well for Telford in pre-season games and he struck me as potentially one of the best crossers of the ball in the Conference. Although we signed him for the season, he played mainly as a substitute and is, at the time of writing, with Hednesford. Another player with Aston Villa connections who did well in pre-season was Michael Blackwood who, a few years earlier, had played alongside Darius Vassell in the successful Aston Villa youth side and was a prolific goalscorer. He had since played for Wrexham, Worcester, Stevenage and Halesowen and won a contract after a spell on trial with Telford. He scored a vital goal in the FA Cup thriller against Tamworth and was a very good passer of the ball, but I felt that he suffered from not being played in a settled position, being used sometimes in attack and sometimes in defence.

Possibly the most exciting of the young signings for Telford, however, was Chris Murphy. I had been impressed when seeing him playing for Shrewsbury reserves, and had talked to Chic Bates about him. When he was released by Shrewsbury in the summer of 2003, soon after Jimmy Quinn had replaced Kevin Ratcliffe as manager, I quickly invited him and his dad to Telford for a chat. He was just about to go on holiday and Mick Jones invited him to come for a pre-season trial on his return. I was surprised at this as I felt that his potential warranted his being signed immediately. I therefore persuaded Mick to offer him a contract there and then. Chris did well in pre-season games and was on the bench for the first two Conference games, and I expected him to battle his way gradually to a first-team place. In fact, by Christmas he was not only in the Telford team but was in the England non-League team together with Sam Ricketts. Chris's success brought back memories of one of my last signings for Hereford, Robert Purdie.

As indicated above, however, not all potential signings come to fruition. There were two players whom Mick Jones had known in his Huddersfield Town days, namely winger Simon Baldry and defender Gareth Evans. Simon looked a particularly good prospect. He had played 166 games for Huddersfield and was still only twenty-eight. Both came to look at accommodation in the Telford area and Evans seemed keen to come, but Baldry decided to sign for Notts County (and in fact won a regular first-team place with them). Evans then seemed to lose interest when he realised that his colleague wasn't coming to Telford. In due course Evans won a contract at Blackpool and played in half of their games in the 2003/04 season, injury causing him to miss the play-off final. Then there was that busy little versatile player Mark Rankine. He had captained Doncaster while still in his teens and I had known him during my Wolves days after his reported £90,000 signing from Doncaster. He has since played over 250 games for Preston, always playing with a smile on his face, but in 2002/03 had been loaned to Sheffield United. After discussions with me with a view to coming to Telford Mark decided that, at thirty-three, he was capable of at least one more season in the Football League and he signed a one-year contract with Sheffield United before moving to Tranmere in time for the 2004/05 season. Much-travelled striker Martin Carruthers, who had begun his career with Aston Villa in 1990, also opted for at least one more season in the Football League when I approached him after he had been released by Scunthorpe. In the event he went to Macclesfield and scored 10 goals for them in 2003/04. I would also like to have signed Rugeley-born defender George Pilkington. He had had several seasons at Everton and was strongly recommended by their former chief executive Michael Dunford, whom I had got to know well when we were both at Derby. George had an impressive loan spell with Exeter in 2002/03 and we had talks with him at the new Bucks Head and arranged for him to come back on the following Saturday and sign for us. We were not very optimistic, however, when, while we were waiting for him to arrive, one of Andy Shaw's staff reported seeing him filling up his car with petrol in Stafford. George later rang in to say that he had signed for Port Vale. In the event he missed only two League games for Vale in 2003/04 and is, at the time of writing, in his third season with them.

One player we did manage to sign during the season, however, was Burton Albion striker Christian Moore. He had begun his career with Leicester and had since then played for several different clubs, but he was still only thirty-one and had scored 18 goals for Burton in the previous season. I felt that he could score lots more goals in the Conference. In the event he had a mixed season for Telford, though he came good with an FA Cup hat-trick against Brentford. Another player signed after the start of the season was Tony Naylor. Initially we hesitated over this thirty-six-year-old former Crewe, Port Vale and Cheltenham striker. Tony, however, proved invaluable with his goals in Telford's FA Trophy run. As someone said at the time, 'A player is not too old if he scores goals in vital games.'

I had had links with the Birmingham Junior side Grosvenor Park when I was at Hereford and two players from there, midfielder Jon Daniels and striker Justin Rowe, had played a few games for Hereford in 2002/03. Both were signed for Telford in the summer of 2003 and there were hopes that they might develop in the course of the season but they enjoyed only limited success. Rowe was loaned to Gresley Rovers near the end of the season and was signed by them after scoring 4 times in 6 games.

All in all 2003/04 was a disappointment for Telford as far as Conference results were concerned. In cup competitions, however, the picture was much brighter, with FA Cup wins over Tamworth, Crawley, Brentford and Crewe before going out to the ultimate finalists Millwall in round four. In the FA Trophy the semi-final was reached before going out to Canvey Island. Serious injuries to Scott Green and Lee Mills didn't help, but right into the New Year I was looking to strengthen the team when players became available. In fact, what proved to be my last signing for Telford was that of Craig Stanley from Walsall in February 2004. I had seen this right-sided midfield player on a number of occasions in the Walsall reserve team and had made a mental note that I would try to sign him if he became available, as he seemed to have considerable potential. He had a successful loan spell with Raith Rovers during the first part of 2003/04 and I was dumbfounded soon afterwards when I saw his name on a list of players Walsall were preparing to release. I could hardly believe my luck and Craig was quickly signed. He made a promising debut as a player with plenty of skill who was always looking to go forward. Soon afterwards, however, came the shattering news that Andy Shaw's business empire had collapsed.

Andy had done tremendous work in providing Telford United with an excellent ground with conference rooms, a leisure centre, swimming pool and gymnasium. A new ninety-bedroom hotel was just being completed. Andy's dream of taking Telford into the Football League had, however, been shattered. It was now a struggle for them to complete the 2003/04 season. Fans rallied magnificently and some hard work behind the scenes saw the fixtures completed and a final position of twelfth in the Conference achieved. Attendances were seventh highest in the Conference, averaging 2,078 compared with 985 in the previous season.

This is not the time to pass judgment on that 2003/04 season, but I shall always be grateful to Andy Shaw for putting his confidence in me and giving me the opportunity to do what I do best, namely unearthing talent, acquiring it and seeking to help to put together a competitive team. Some fans said that the players brought in did not all fulfil their potential. They didn't. Some said that the state of the pitch, which was waterlogged at times, was a factor in the mediocre league position. It wasn't. Several other reasons were put forward, but the real reason was that not enough points were gained. That there was enough ability at the club was indicated by the excellent displays against Shrewsbury Town.

I was very disappointed by the events of spring 2004 when the club as it was then nearly folded and the team on the field failed to win anything tangible after at one stage being in the running for a place in the Football League, the FA Trophy and considerable progress in the FA Cup. Injuries to key players such as Lee Mills and Scott Green did not help and when it came to priorities it did seem at one time that not all were singing from the same hymn sheet.

Under the label AFC Telford the re-formed team has now progressed to one division below the second division of the Conference. Officials of the original Telford club (including myself) are no longer with the club but I shall always remember the tremendous work of people like Mike Ferriday, Rob Cave and Paul Booth, the high level of hospitality and organisation and the way Andy Shaw provided one of the best non-League pitches and one of the best non-League grounds.

TEN

# CHANGES IN MY TIME

*Responsibility can sometimes break a strong man down.*

*Responsibility can sometimes drag a weak man to his feet.*

When I came into professional scouting in 1957 the Football League consisted of the First and Second Divisions and the Northern and Southern sections of the Third Division. The reorganisation of the two Third Division sections into the Third and Fourth Divisions was imminent, but there was no hint of a Premier League or a Football Conference that would offer automatic promotion to the Football League to the winners. Wolves had just stirred the nation's hearts with exciting victories over top European clubs in floodlit friendlies and plans were being laid for a European Cup competition. The World Cup had been in existence since 1930, but there was no European Championship and England *v.* Scotland games were regarded by most fans both sides of the border as the most important international clashes in the calendar. Sendings-off were relatively rare and anyone who suggested that handling the ball or celebrating a goal would ultimately become a dismissible offence would have been laughed at. In fact, there have been more changes in the last few decades than at any time since the late nineteenth century, when string was replaced by a crossbar and handling the ball was limited to goalkeepers. Some of the changes in recent years have been for the better but others I would love to reverse and get back to how things were when I played the game as a teenager.

How lovely it would be to have Saturday 3 p.m. kick-offs again for both first team and reserves so that fans would know that there was a game at their ground at that time every week from August to April. Many other fans would agree with this. As things are, television and police have combined (or rather worked independently) to have weekend games played at a variety of times from Friday evening to Monday evening, with even the odd game at Boxing Day teatime. Certainly the fact that reserve games are played at any time other than Saturday afternoons and usually at a distance from home grounds has meant that the 'first team one week and reserves the next' type of fan has disappeared and clubs seem at times almost to discourage reserve team watching by giving little publicity to games, changing days and kick-off times at short notice and often playing games miles away from the club's home grounds. In recent seasons Walsall reserves have borrowed Hednesford's ground on occasion in order to fulfil some of their 'home' fixtures. Why? Because their own Bescot Stadium is being used by Aston Villa reserves. Finance has been an important factor in such anomalies, as it has been in many of the changes in the game over the years. Another result of reserve games being played almost anywhere within a twenty-five-mile radius of a club's home ground is that players who do not appear in the first team may spend a whole season with a club without ever playing on the club's home ground. This can mean that a young player making his debut in the first team may find he is just as much a stranger to his club's home ground as he would be if playing away.

Even more serious is the fact that the development of schools of excellence has meant that boys can be plucked to join them almost as soon as they start school and can be turned away at an early age as seeming failures. With schools of excellence taking players at a younger and younger age, schoolboy football has declined dramatically and this situation has been aggravated by the development of teachers' contracts, so that there is no longer a body of unsung and unpaid heroes voluntarily running school teams, mainly in their own time. The fact that many secondary schools (some of then now labelled sports colleges) now include a wider rage of sports in the curriculum – tennis, hockey, golf, canoeing, mountaineering etc, means that in some cases football has a lower profile than in the days when football, cricket and swimming were just about the only sports practised in schools.

The modern craze for computer games also means that boys spend less time out on a local patch of ground kicking a ball about with coats for goalposts, as was the case a generation and more ago. How many football-ers of yesteryear learned their basic skills that way? This may also have a relevance to present-day concerns about children's obesity. It is one of the ironies that, in an era when Schools of Excellence proliferate, fewer boys play football in playgrounds and parks just for fun. Parents with big bucks before their eyes now have visions of their offspring becoming footballers, whereas previous generations of parents had dreams of the medical or legal professions for their children. Boys making it through to become professional footballers will inevitably always be in a minority, and the situation has been aggravated in recent years by the influx of foreign players who take the places in Football League teams formerly occupied by home-grown talent. A number of clubs, particularly those in the Premier League, regularly field teams more than half of which consist of foreign players. Rarely now does one see the headline 'local boy makes good' and when young boys have dreams of playing profes-sional football it is not necessarily for their local club. One only has to catch a glimpse of replica shirts on washing lines to realise that far more lads today are wearing the colours of the Manchester Uniteds, Arsenals and Chelseas rather than those of their local clubs. Many, moreover, are merely television supporters, and have never seen their favourite clubs 'in the flesh' so to speak.

While the influx of overseas players is not limited to football, one feels that the cricket authorities have handled the situation rather more pur-posefully in limiting the number of overseas players that a club can have on its books at any one time. Even so, many cricket devotees still claim that imports from overseas have had a negative effect on the development of home-grown talent and ultimately on the England team. As write I am pleased to note the improved results that the England team has achieved in the recent series against the West Indies, New Zealand, South Africa and Australia. It would be nice to think that something could be done to encourage the flow of native talent and give the England football team real hope of winning something in the foreseeable future.

I also find it rather sad that clubs change the appearance of their shirts most seasons, thus vastly increasing the cost for parents of providing their children with up-to-date replica kits. While on the subject of shirts, I can remember the pre-war days when teams did not wear numbers and it was a delight to me when, in 1939, numbered shirts were introduced with each position on the field having its own particular number, from goalkeepers wearing number one to left wingers wearing number eleven. These numbers became meaningful and even when substitutes were introduced in 1965 one became used to the number twelve and then the number fourteen coming on. Now, with the squad systems and each player having a number that, other things being equal, he keeps throughout the season, fans are more confused than ever. The numbers on the backs mean little or nothing and even with names now added, fans are often more puzzled as to who is who and playing where than in the pre-war games when shirts were un-numbered. Still on the subject of kit, the tendency to change away kits seasonally is not helpful to travelling fans, who in the past found a security and identity in knowing what their favourites would look like when they ran out.

When I first watched football before, during and just after the Second World War there was a continuous call for substitutes to be allowed for injured players and one recalls several FA Cup finals being marred by serious injuries that almost certainly affected the result. Arsenal's Wally Barnes, Bolton's Eric Bell, Manchester City's Jimmy Meadows, Nottingham Forest's Roy Dwight and Blackburn's Dave Whelan all suffered serious injuries in FA Cup finals between 1952 and 1960 and all except Roy Dwight ended on the losing side. Though Manchester City goalkeeper Bert Trautmann played on in the 1956 final after breaking a bone in his neck and ended up on the winning side, the feeling was that, in so doing, he had put his very life at risk. The argument then was that if substitutes were allowed for injured players teams might take advantage by a player being encouraged to feign injury if he was off form. The manager could then replace him with a substitute. In fact, when eventually substitutes were allowed (in 1965 in League games and in 1966 in FA Cup ties) they could only officially be allowed in cases of injury. How far away that seems to be now when each team can name up to five substitutes and use any three in a game. This has produced something of a tactical revolution with certain players being used more often as substitutes than for whole games. Just occasionally a manager uses his three substitutes and then finds one of his team struggling with an injury, so that he is left with just ten fit men on the field. There is no doubt, however, that the introduction of substitutes has improved the game. On the other hand, one would not be happy if the current number was increased so that one had the ridiculous situation, as in certain international friendly games, of a completely different team ending the game from that which began it.

If the introduction of substitutes has improved the game in my time then so has the arrival of floodlights. Very primitive lights (virtually bulbs on the end of long poles) were tried way back in the last century, but it wasn't until improved technology after the Second World War that they became a practical proposition. When Wolves beat teams like Spartak Moscow and Honved in the mid-1950s the whole nation responded, not just to the fact that an English club was taking on and beating some of the best club sides in the world, but to the sense that floodlights brought a particularly exciting atmosphere to the ground. It was not until February 1956 that floodlights were first permitted for a Football League game (Portsmouth *v.* Newcastle being the first) but it was clear from that point on that they were here to stay and they have certainly made it possible for clubs to have fixture lists balanced throughout the season rather than in the days when evening games could only be played at the beginning and end of seasons, as any midweek games in between suffered from poor gates when played in an afternoon.

Mention of floodlights, however, inevitably brings television into the equation. Television has brought a great deal of money into the game and it is interesting how things have changed from the days when televising live games was thought of as destructive to the whole fabric of football in that it would keep people away from grounds. Now money has talked and, while efforts are made to prevent televised games clashing with a whole programme of League or cup games, one now finds a surfeit of football at various levels on the screen. This automatically creates a large number of 'television' fans, as opposed to those who, over the years, have witnessed matches at first hand. While television does a great job in making the watching of a game available to the elderly and infirm who just can't physically attend games, it is unfortunate that many who are capable of attending are finding it more comfortable and more convenient to watch from their armchairs.

Talking of comfort, one has had to come to terms with all-seater stadia in the light of the Taylor Report that followed the Hillsborough disaster of 1989. While standing spectators are still accommodated at non-League and lower division grounds it is no longer possible to watch top-level foot-ball 'from the terraces'. This, combined with vastly increased admission prices, has changed football from a mainly working-class entertainment to a mainly middle-class one. In addition there is now a new phenomenon of television fans who watch games on Sky and then ring local radio stations to give their opinions on the game. I cannot really accept such people as fans if they never visit a football ground to savour the special atmosphere of a game.

Happily, every club does still have its hardcore fans who watch their favourites home and away, game by game, even though it becomes increas-ingly difficult to afford the admission prices and to fit one's life around the variety of kick-off times that are dictated on the one hand by television requirements and on the other hand by the police. No longer can a fan buy a season ticket sure in the knowledge that there will be either a first team or reserve team game at his local ground on a Saturday at 3 p.m. and that other games will be on a weekday evening. While many fans continue to support their clubs through highs and lows year in year out, it is sad that no longer do players in general show the same dedication to a club. Nowadays one does not have a John Trollope playing 770 games for his one and only club (Swindon Town) or a Roy Sproson turning out 761 times for Port Vale. Nor are there international players these days who spend their whole careers with one club as Billy Wright (Wolves), Jimmy Dickenson (Portsmouth) and Gil Merrick (Birmingham) did in the two decades after the Second World War. Contracts are now of varying lengths rather than season by season but may become meaningless as players (or in many cases their agents) seek new contracts a year or more before the old one has expired, with the lever that, if their contract expires, they are free to negotiate with a new club without their present club receiving any fee for their services.

Together with the virtual disappearance of the one-club man, one now rarely sees the sort of 'play anywhere' utility man that was popular with most clubs in the years before and after the Second World War. One thinks of Leeds' John Charles, an international in both defence and attack, and Portsmouth's Jack Froggatt, who played both on the left flank of the attack and in the defence for England, while men like Birmingham's Don Dearson, Aston Villa's Harry Parkes and Walsall's Colin Harrison all played first-team football successfully in defence, midfield and attack.

If one seems to be singing forever that 'Fings Ain't Wot They Used T'be', it can be pointed out that the FA Cup is still the major domestic competition with its special thrills for clubs at all levels. While this great competition does happily still exist, even this has lost some of its traditional excitement. Sponsorship has not quite taken away its traditional label, but the 2004 competition was labelled as being in partnership with Nationwide, which seems just one step away from going the same way as the Scottish Cup, which has now become the Tennants Scottish Cup. Sadly, FA Cup days are no longer characterised by all games kicking off at 3 p.m. on the Saturday but are more of an FA Cup weekend, with ties played at any time from Friday evening to Monday evening. Nor is the draw at a specific time, but tends to be made later on the Saturday afternoon, with some ties complete and some still to be played. No longer is there the weekend's excitement that there once was when a 'little' team, having pulled off a giant-killing act on the Saturday, spent all day Sunday savouring the possibility of a really glamorous draw as they waited for the Monday lunchtime draw to be made. There is, however, still a certain magic to this competition that began way back in 1872 and embraces hundreds of clubs with the extra preliminary round played in September and the final taking place over eight months later. While teams such as Manchester United have made it clear that they regard European competition as far more important, European competitions involve only a handful of Premiership clubs so that, for most clubs, the FA Cup is still the greatest competition in the world and, as Millwall showed recently, a comparatively small club can still battle through to the final.

Captaincy of teams is one aspect of the game that happily has not changed very much over the years. I have appreciated the importance of a captain to a side since I first watched games before the Second World War and admired the skippers. Their importance is just as great today. Just before and just after the Second World War, Wolves' Stan Cullis was one who stood out as a captain, both playing well himself and getting the best out of his team. The captain has always seemed to me to be an extension of the manager's influence carried onto the field of play. In both football and cricket I have long felt that a good captain can be worth his place in a team for his captaincy alone, quite apart from his contribution as a player. In the 1950s and 1960s, both before and after Oxford United achieved Football League status, Ron Atkinson was an inspiration to all around him. He led his team by exhortation and example. So too did Benny Fenton in his days at Colchester in the mid-1950s. He had made his debut for West Ham nearly twenty years earlier but, even as his fortieth birthday approached, Benny was tactically as sharp as a needle, getting the best out of his men. He was at that time both manager and captain of the U's and literally carried the influence of the manager onto the field of play. Not all good captains make good managers, but one who certainly has done is Brian Horton, the Midlands lad who captained Port Vale, Luton and Brighton in the 1970s and 1980s and has recently completed his thousandth game as a manager, with clubs ranging from Manchester City to his current club Macclesfield. One thing I would like to be more respected in general is the captain's armband. He should surely be the only player allowed to query a referee's decision, but many players chat back on their own account and not all referees are prepared to give an answer if a captain asks why a particular decision has been made.

A scout, as has become abundantly clear in looking back over my time in the game, has his ups and downs and needs something to sustain him on the days when things are not going well. One obvious source of encouragement, particularly on a bitterly cold day as he travels the length and breadth of the country, is the hospitality he receives from clubs visited. While most clubs provide a half-time cup of tea, others go the extra mile with refreshments before and after a game. Of the 'big' clubs, I have found Coventry, Leicester and Wolves to be particularly hospitable in my area and further afield Manchester United and Newcastle are two other clubs who excel. Of the newer clubs, one always feels particularly well received at Rushden & Diamonds and Kidderminster. On the other hand, one does not feel over-indulged at West Bromwich, where scouts do not always find themselves in a seat that gives a clear view of play. In fact I have known an Arsenal scout leave The Hawthorns in the first half after watching a game from a poor vantage point sitting next to or near the corner flag. I also have unhappy memories of a 400-mile round trip to a game at Plymouth where I received no hospitality and was allocated a seat near to the back of a stand surrounded by vociferous so-called fans. The reaction of clubs whose scout is not particularly well looked after on a visit to another ground varies enormously. Some try to ensure that the rather lukewarm welcome is reciprocated when they are visited by a representative of the less-than-hospitable club. Others try to embarrass their opposite number by giving generous hospitality in the hope that their own scouts will be better received on subsequent visits. 'Do unto others', as the Good Book says.

It is interesting that, while clubs will automatically provide tickets to scouts for League games provided that a request is made in advance by phone or fax, cup ties are a different matter, 'Everyone Pays' notices are often posted, the only exceptions normally being that scouts of opponents over the next few weeks are provided for.

Personally speaking, I have particularity appreciated the hospitality provided by lower division and non-League clubs such as Rochdale, Hednesford and Moor Green, the pies at Rochdale's Spotland ground and at Kidderminster's Aggborough being particularly good. It is always good to show one's appreciation at non-League grounds by buying a raffle ticket and on the few occasions that my ticket has come out of the hat I have taken pleasure in giving the prize back to be re-raffled, thus helping the club funds just a little. Most clubs realise that treating a visiting scout well can be an investment as they may at a future date be seeking a favour from the scout's club. As in other walks of life, one can't put a price on goodwill when it comes to relationships between football clubs. The fact that some clubs do not pay attention to encouraging visiting scouts may mean that the humble scout finds himself among fans at the back of a very long queue and paying for his cup of tea.

Sometimes of course a scout may visit a ground incognito and among many 'anonymous' visits to grounds I have particular memories of a soaking on a wet might at Nuneaton already referred to when Graham Turner and I went to watch Bournemouth's Neil Masters in an FA Cup replay. I also recall turning up my coat collar and paying for admission on a number of occasions at Halesowen's Abbey Stadium. On one occasion I met Halesowen's secretary Harry Rudge (one of the game's unsung heroes). He said to me, 'Haven't seen you at Halesowen recently,' and my ready response was, 'You haven't looked in the right place, Harry.'

Thinking of experiences as a scout travelling around different grounds, there are some that were not funny at the time but raise a smile when looking back. I recall Ray Shaw in his later days as chief scout of Leicester City asking me to watch Coventry reserves against Liverpool reserves at Highfield Road as a favour to him. I was between jobs at the time and I parked in the street ready for a speedy getaway at the end of the game. Having some time to spare before kick-off (or so I thought) I dozed off, only to be awoken by a member of the Coventry Constabulary tapping on the car window. He politely asked, 'Are you all right Sir?' 'I'm here to see the reserve game against Liverpool,' was my confident reply. 'That will be difficult Sir,' was his immediate response, 'the game was played last night.' Not to be deprived of seeing a game I immediately started the car and headed along the A444 to Nuneaton's Manor Park, where I was very impressed by home defender Kirk Stephens. I immediately informed Ray Shaw, but other people must also have known of Stephens' potential as, shortly afterwards, he was signed by David Pleat (himself a former Nuneaton man) who was then at Luton.

I also found the dedication of fellow scouts a great help in keeping my spirits up. In my Walsall days there were up to a dozen scouts, all operating in the Midlands. I think of Freddy Whittall, a former non-League player who travelled by bus to most of his assignments and who recommended defender Mick Evans, then of Vono Sports. Then there was Stan Parkes, a West Bromwich Albion fan living in Tipton, who was a cousin of former Albion and Villa defender Jimmy Dugdale. He, like several others, special- ised in watching schoolboy football on Saturday mornings. So did George Wiggins, who lived in Pelsall. I think also of Bob Williamson, secretary of the Staffordshire FA and very well known in the Cannock, Brownhills and Lichfield area. He had recommended prolific pre-war striker Billy Evans to Walsall in the 1930s and was still going strong in the 1960s. Walsall were particularly well served in the Cannock area at that time with Eric Sanders, a one-time Walsall reserve goalkeeper and Charlie Wright (whom I have referred to in a previous chapter) also operating there. Of the scouts I worked with in my Shrewsbury days reference has been made in a previous chapter to Harry Maney, the school caretaker who recommended a steady flow of players from his Newton Albion team. He later succeeded me as Shrewsbury chief scout and later still went on to work with Chic Bates and Lou Macari at Swindon and Stoke. He was very knowledgeable and hardworking. At Derby, and later at Wolves, Ken Guttridge stood out as a most knowledgeable and conscientious scout. Numerous ex-players served as scouts at Derby, often when 'between jobs', so to speak, and in this connection names such as David Nish, Bruce Rioch and Henry Newton immediately spring to mind, not forgetting former Walsall midfielder Ken Hodgkisson who loved scouting but was less efficient at sending in match reports. Talking of reports, none did them better than Bill Clayton, who worked with me at both Derby and Hereford and is at the time of writing working for Preston. Wolves used lots of local scouts, among them Geoff Blackwell, a most efficient and enthusiastic recruiter of schoolboy talent for the centre of excellence, and Tony Painter, who later moved to work with Robert Kelly at Blackburn. Of scouts with whom I worked at Hereford I was lucky that, when Bill Clayton moved on, he was succeeded by Alan Brookes, who also wrote excellent match reports. Alan followed me to Telford in 2003 and Telford scouts during my time there included Mick Evans, who had been signed by me as a young player some forty years earlier.

Some scouts have memorable sayings. I think of Eric Houghton, the former Aston Villa player, manager and director, who, during his time as a director at Walsall, also did some scouting. On the subject of full-backs Eric's words stuck in my mind from the first time I heard them: 'Don't sign small full-backs. Send them to Aintree to be jockeys.'

Closely linked with scouts are the club secretaries and other behind-the-scenes people at smaller clubs, whose names are indelibly linked with that particular club. Such people can raise the image of a club simply by being the people they are. Until his death a few years ago Harry Rudge personified Halesowen Town. While I was at Walsall I encouraged Harry to sign one of our reserve defenders Dave Culwick, who went on to be a key figure in the Halesowen defence for many years. Harry, meanwhile, had a hand in one of his players, Norman Rowe, moving to Walsall – and Norman went on to play for the Saddlers in two memorable FA Cup games against Fulham in 1962. Harry's distinctive figure could be seen on the Halesowen touchline in all weathers, always urging his side on in between the many jobs he did behind the scenes, always aware that, however hard everyone may be trying on and off the field, only one side could win the league. In fact Harry brought the famous lines of Rudyard Kipling to mind, being able to face triumph and disaster with equal resolve and keep pressing on.

Just as one automatically associates Harry Rudge with Halesowen one thinks of similar people working in similar ways at other clubs. Such an example is Alan Parsons at Boldmere St Michaels, a man who has built team after team over the years with many of his players being snapped up by teams in higher leagues. What a tribute to his talent-spotting ability. Not very far from Boldmere, Rob Faulkner at Moor Green has always fostered good football on one of the best playing surfaces in the Midlands at The Moorlands. How sad that at the time of writing, vandals have forced Moor Green to move temporarily from their own ground.

When I think of the dedicated men keeping the wheels turning at clubs rarely in the limelight, my mind turns to George Mycock at Walsall Wood going around on his cycle to deliver invitations to players chosen for the next game, or Sid Baker at Walsall Trinity putting up the goal nets or pouring the half-time tea. Both incidentally wore flat caps as a ready reminder of the working-class background that they shared with so many fans of that era. The efficiency and enthusiasm of such men was all part of their character underpinned by a love for the game. As this book is being produced one hears sadly of the death of Fred Whittall who, for many years, had links with Walsall Football Club, always submitting his reports on Monday morning, always making approaches to other clubs in the proper manner. What ambassadors for their clubs and for the game in general such men were.

As we think of unsung heroes we think of those who have their moments of glory in the midst of many years of routine unspectacular service. In 1997 John Baldwin led Hednesford Town to a fourth round FA Cup tie at Middlesbrough, where they actually took the lead and finally went down to a narrow 3-2 defeat. In his time John had served the club in a variety of roles, including those of goalkeeper, manager and chairman. I remember him from his days as a young goalkeeper in the Walsall youth team.

Think of consistent service and one thinks of groundsmen at well-known and less well-known clubs. Albert Tye maintained the pitch at Molineux before and after the Second World War, often responding to the sometimes idiosyncratic requests of manager Major Frank Buckley who, on occasions, had the Molineux pitch watered on sunny days since at that time his players' superior stamina worked to best effect in heavy conditions. In a later era Bill Pilbeam was another outstanding Wolves groundsman, a great character with green fingers and many stories to tell. I have heard most of them at one time or another, several of them many times over. Then, until his retirement a few years ago, Roger Johnson served Walsall (and for a time Birmingham City) as groundsman with a combination of up-to-date skills, dedication and common sense. Men like this are to be found up and down the country though rarely known by name outside their own club.

Nor are the names of club secretaries usually known by fans in general, though they are often the people who make a club tick by doing 101 jobs ranging from the drawing up of contracts to the checking of gate receipts and seeking sponsors. In between these activities such men and women are forever making and receiving telephone calls. On match days secretaries are busy with such a range of activities they rarely see much of the game itself. One thinks of Terry Brumpton at Hednesford, Mike Ferriday, formerly of Telford, Ernie Lamb, formerly of Rushall Olympic, Hugh Clarke at Stourbridge and his near neighbours Messrs Tildesley and Ewing. Such men are at least as vital to their respective clubs as any Premier League secretary.

Moving to sponsors, this has been a growth area in the last twenty or so years and they have to some extent eased the pressure on club benefactors, though there are still the super-fans who bankroll clubs. One of the best known of these in recent years has been the late Jack Walker at Blackburn, while I have seen at first hand the major inputs of Sir Jack Haywood at Wolves, Andy Shaw at Telford and Steve Price at Hednesford. Financial inputs to clubs are also made by supporters' clubs, where groups of unsung heroes and heroines keep raising funds year in, year out. During the whole of my time at Walsall people like Sam Canning, Bernard Johnston, Elsie Siddons and John Wilson worked tirelessly and at times income from the supporters' clubs eased severe crises when the secretary of that time Ernie Wilson hunted round in order to pay the players' wages.

Every club also owes much to its tea ladies, who provide efficient service with a smile and promote goodwill to visitors. I think of Brenda,

Julie and Janet at Hednesford, typifying so many ladies up and down the country. Then there are the laundry ladies like Mrs Clamp at Wolves. She has now retired and is best known as the mother of a former Wolves and England midfielder, the late Eddie Clamp. She and so many more are deserving of the highest respect and gratitude.

At the heart of football, however, are those teachers who over the years have organised school teams, giving freely of their spare time to coach young players and select and accompany school teams. Many of the players I have signed over the years have come from this source. I think among others of Tom Pugh (Cannock), Roger Jaques (Nuneaton), Bob Davidson (South-East Staffs), George Pearson (Brierley Hill), Martin Duffield (Brierley Hill and National Executive), Bob Thomas (Walsall), Barry Austin (Wolverhampton), Harry Davenhill (Brownhills), John Appleby (Burton) and Bob Ellis (Telford). I have been lucky to meet such people, just as I have been lucky to meet some of the household names in the game. Bertie Mee and Tommy Docherty at different times offered me jobs at Arsenal and Aston Villa respectively, while at one time I was on an FA Working Party with such names as Dario Gradi, Jimmy Hill and Rick Parry. It was a privilege and an education to be in their presence and I still savour the forthright views articulated by Dario Gradi, currently far and away the longest-serving manager in the Football League, having been at Gresty Road since 1983. He is a real character.

Underpinning all the well-known and lesser-known people in the game, however, are the fans. While writing this chapter I broke off to read the current issue of the *Sports Argus*, the Saturday evening paper that I was first thrilled to read as a boy. Under the heading 'Cost of Living Dream Tests Loyalty of Football Devotees' the writer makes the comment that 'in the world of corporate hospitality, executive boxes, pre-match presentations etc, it is the all-too-often forgotten long-suffering fans who have to cough up for match tickets that ultimately pay the wages of the players.' He goes on to point out that for the 2004/05 season Spurs fans will be paying as much as £1,265 for a season ticket and that the total cost to a fan for travelling to and gaining admission to an away game can be as much as £100 for just one game. While fans don't look for medals for such sacrifices it does bring home the fact that players should appreciate the type of people that they are playing for and always give of their best.

My career in football began as a player and junior secretary with Walsall YMCA in the Walsall Minor League at grass-roots level with the unsung heroes of the game. As I approach my fiftieth year as a scout, I am doing a little work with a Southern League Premier club. I still find it a real joy to be involved and I still get daily requests from all over the country for information on players. Maybe the wheel has come full circle. I do, however, miss being focussed on a particular club where I can have a positive input. I have now been in the game in one way or another for sixty-two years. I hope I can achieve a few more.

# THEY SAY ABOUT RON

COLIN ADDISON (former Arsenal and Sheffield United player and Hereford, West Bromwich Albion and Yeovil manager): I have known Ron Jukes a very long time. In my first spell at Hereford in the early 1970s he would turn up at all sorts of grounds, well known and almost unknown. Whenever we bumped into each other we always had a few minutes' chat about this player and that and over the years we have kept in touch. I have always found Ron's judgment to be impeccable. It is almost an understatement to say that he knew a player when he saw one. In looking at a young player he has always looked for character as well as skill. Without the former, the latter can never come to fruition.

GRAHAM ALLNER (former manager of Kidderminster, AP Leamington and Cheltenham): Mention of Ron Jukes takes my mind back some thirty-five years to a chilly Sunday afternoon at Henry Road Playing Fields in Birmingham. I was playing for Brookhill, who were about to become a nursery team to Walsall and Ron, then a chief scout of high repute at Fellows Park, came to run the rule over us. I had a stinker and afterwards was distraught at blowing my chance until the manager said Ron wanted a word. When the nursery club announcement was made a few days later it included news that I was to be Walsall's first signing under the arrangement. I have always insisted, tongue firmly in cheek, that it was down to Ron's innate ability to spot talent, but his record down the years bears out that claim. A talented youth team at Walsall that year was all Ron's work and our goalkeeper Phil Parkes went on to star for QPR, West Ham and England.

Years later, football management took me to many football outposts looking for players and Ron was often there searching out another 'nugget' for clubs such as Shrewsbury, Derby, Wolves, Hereford and Telford. Today, as blunt and gruff as ever, he is still at it nearly fifty years on and I among many others still value highly his knowledge, assessment and advice, but above all his friendship.

RON ATKINSON (former Oxford player, Cambridge, West Bromwich Albion, Aston Villa and Manchester United manager and television pundit): As a chief scout, Ron Jukes is every manager's dream. Always ready to watch any player anywhere, in a large stadium or on a parks pitch, he always comes back with a straight tale – a player can either play or he can't. Ron follows in the tradition of the good old club scouts such as George Noakes, who was for so many years with Wolves and who incidentally took both Ron and myself to Molineux as lads.

NICK ATTHEY (over 500 games for Walsall): I was signed by Ron in 1961 as a schoolboy after he had seen me playing for Coventry Schools. Ron brought to Walsall at that time players like Allan Clarke, Phil Parkes and Mark Wallington, who went on to win international or representative honours, but I personally believe he got as much pleasure out of watching players such as Stan Bennett, Frank Gregg, Colin Harrison, Mick Evans and myself who between us played nearly 2,000 games for Walsall. Many a Sunday afternoon you would see Ron watching games on King George's Playing Fields, Bloxwich. His enthusiasm for the game is as strong now as it was then. My wife and I have always valued the friendship of Ron and his wife Molly. Thanks Ron.

JOHN BALDWIN (former Hednesford player, manager and chairman, now director at Kidderminster): When I think of Ron, one word comes to mind – KNOWLEDGE. There is not a player playing that he does not have an intimate knowledge of, and he is always willing to help you with his opinion and advice. The only exception to this is if he is interested in the same player, then he tends to have a selective memory. So many people involved in football owe Ron so much. His ability to spot a player is second to none, plus he is a thoroughly nice guy.

CHIC BATES (former Shrewsbury player and manager): In the spring of 1968 Ron Jukes came to my parents' home in West Bromwich. He was already very well known as Walsall FC chief scout and his reputation for spotting football talent was immense. He wanted me to talk with the Walsall management of that time with a view to signing for them. To my regret and Ron's this never quite happened.

In June 1984 I became manager of Shrewsbury Town. The chief scout was Ron Jukes, who was fantastic at finding players. He never let me down. In 2004 he is still talking and asking me about players. His enthusiasm and knowhow in his search for players must make him one of the best chief scouts over the past fifty years.

COLIN BEECH (on behalf of North Walsall Old Boys): Ron had an eye for talent in the 1950s. Most of us were lucky to have him as a sports master. There was no time for boredom when Ron was around. After lessons it was cricket, swimming, football, football and more football. Blending a school team from an early age – that was Ron's aim. One of Ron's lads (Kenny Hill) had a professional career with Walsall and Norwich. Ron's scouting talent brought many potential top-class players to his beloved Walsall Football Club and later to other clubs. We have been proud to know this gentleman.

STAN BENNETT (over 500 games for Walsall): The first time I met Ron Jukes was my last day of school. I had never considered a career in football, even though a number of clubs had been watching me for a long time. Ron convinced me that I give it a try and I became a Walsall Football Club player. I realised what a marvellous talent spotter Ron was when

I was seventeen, the captain of the youth team and in an early round of the youth cup. We were drawn against West Bromwich Albion away, the First Division favourites who had a team of ex-schoolboy internationals and major starlets. We, by comparison, had a team that were all found by Ron. We won and were by far the better side on the night.

Looking back, nine of that side went on to play for the first team. The most amazing skill Ron has is to find people with a talent for football in all departments, defenders, midfielders and attackers. In my eighteen years in football I can think of over fifty players that Ron found. He also found many, many more before and after my time. I would just love to know how many players Ron actually found and exactly what it is that he looks for.

I would like to thank Ron for eighteen years of fun and for seeing something in me that I am still unable to see.

GEOFF BLACKWELL (former Wolves, Derby and Hereford scout): I worked with Ron at three different clubs and can say unreservedly that he was the shrewdest scout I ever met. His thinking was always a few moves in front of everyone else and I shall always remember some of his one-liners, such as 'follow your nose' when sending me on a scouting mission. In his mid-seventies, Ron's razor-keen mind is as sharp as ever. He is a generous man in every sense of the word.

DAVID BROWN (former Warwickshire and England Test cricketer): Ron was one of the greatest enthusiasts I have had the privilege of being involved with in sport. I first met him when I was at school and the amount of time he put into out-of-hours coaching and encouragement would not be contemplated in schools nowadays. Apart from my father, he was the first person to encourage me to play cricket, even if at Bluecoat Junior School, Walsall, he thought I was a wicketkeeper-batsman, a thought I shared at the time. He also found time to nurture our swimming and soccer, albeit with very limited success in my case. I have no doubt that if hang gliding and bungee jumping had been in fashion he would have included them too.

I also had the pleasure of playing cricket with and against Ron in later life when I was playing for Walsall against Blakenall and occasionally when I played for Blakenall. Ron was a most determined and accomplished batsman who sold his wicket dearly, as I know to my cost, as I had by then become a fast bowler.

I would like to say a sincere thank you to Ron for the start he gave me on the road to a cricket career and also for the help he has given to countless other sportsmen.

TERRY BRUMPTON (chief executive, Hednesford Town FC): I have met Ron Jukes many times over the years as he has visited Hednesford both at the old Cross Keys Ground and the new Keys Park. Whether he was scouting for Walsall, Birmingham, Shrewsbury, Derby, Wolves, Hereford or Telford he always showed an astounding knowledge of League and non-League football. It was said of him that he could talk for England – but always the talk was underpinned by an amazing eye for talent. Even at the age of seventy-six he is hyperactive, never missing a follow-up when in pursuit of a player. It is always a revelation when discussing football matters with him.

ALAN BUCKLEY (205 goals in 483 games for Walsall and former Walsall, Grimsby, West Bromwich Albion and Lincoln manager):

RON THE MAN

I'm sure you've seen him down the Rec
At Rushall, Wednesbury, even the Pleck
The man who was Walsall's chief scout
A local headmaster – he certainly got about

Football crazy, football mad
His eye for a player wasn't bad
Watching games till it got dark
As he brought the best lads to Fellows Park

Then it happened one sad day
Graham Turner took him to the Meadow Gay
The man certainly clocked up the miles
Adding names of players to his files

Then came a spell at Derby County
With great success we all agree
Renewing a friendship with Arthur Cox
This football scout cunning as a fox

Then back with Graham at Molineux
When Garry Pendrey was there too
Promotion from Fourth to the Second Division
With players spotted by you know who

To find so many players – what a feat
And then came a spell at Edgar Street
And from there on to the new Bucks Head
Pursuing talent as his sixth sense led

The man – Ron Jukes is his name
Football is his life, his game
In his scouting ability I'm a believer
And we've both got a soft spot for a golden retriever

STEVE BULL (over 300 goals for Wolves and 5 England caps): Ron Jukes was the man who, in November 1986, said to Graham Turner, 'Get young Bull over here', after seeing me playing for Albion reserves. Ever since then I have been saying 'Thanks Ron, for picking me up when my career was at the crossroads.' A gentle giant, loved and respected by all, Ron is the man I have contacted over the years when I have had a problem. We have had many conversations and have never had a cross word. Ron is a man who is always as good as his word. What you see is what you get. I am lucky to have met him.

PHIL CANNING (former Blakenall cricketer and non-League footballer): I have known Ron Jukes for over half a century. He has always loved football and cricket equally and has a thorough knowledge of both games. When I was bowling spinners for Blakenall he time and again held catches in the deep field. That sums Ron up – a safe pair of hands in whatever he does.

BRIAN CASWELL (454 games for Walsall before spells with Doncaster and Leeds): Ron Jukes was my schoolmaster when I attended Mesty Croft School, Wednesbury. He was a large, intimidating man with a booming voice – but his bark was worse than his bite.

It was nearly forty years ago that he approached me with the words 'Can you catch a ball?' When I replied in the affirmative he put me in goal, despite the fact that I was the smallest boy in the team and other schools seemed to put their biggest lad in that position. Soon goals were flying past me but then, in the final of the Wednesbury Charity Cup, I pulled off a terrific save in the last minute and we won 1-0. Ron's judgment had paid off.

Mr Jukes, as I knew him, was a fine teacher, an excellent headmaster and a great talent spotter with a knack of recognising a potential Football League player after watching him for a mere ten minutes – his record over the years proves this. I thank him most sincerely for all he taught me.

ALLAN CLARKE (former Walsall, Fulham and Leicester player, player and manager of Leeds, 10 goals in 19 games for England): I first met Ron when I was still at school. All the West Midlands clubs seemed to be inter-ested in me at the time and Aston Villa manager Joe Mercer had taken me to Villa Park for training and he had given me two complimentary tickets for each home game. It was Ron's persistence, however, that convinced me that Walsall was the club for me.

Walsall FC owe a big debt to Ron for bringing through not only myself but many other future Football League players. I would like to place on record my own personal thanks to him. I couldn't have started with a better club and I would also like to say a big thankyou to everyone involved with me during my time at Walsall FC.

MATTHEW CLARKE (former Wolves, Kidderminster, Hereford and Telford player, now at Redditch): It was a great shock to me, an Albion fan, to be asked by Ron Jukes to link up with Wolves, but it is something I have never regretted. I was lucky enough to be linked with Ron at three different clubs and since then he has always been available almost any time of the day or night to make or receive phone calls. It is always good to talk to him – and he has never varied all the time I have known him, whether in his appearance or the soundness of his judgment.

BILL CLAYTON (former Hereford and Preston scout): Ron was quite simply the man who gave me my chance, and took me out of junior football to Wolves, Derby and Hereford. He opened up so many doors for me, including the amazing experience of working for Kevin Keegan at Fulham.

He loves Midlanders and players whose character he knows he can trust. He is at his very best when he has little money to spend. He is hard but fair, and very supportive (especially when he helped me through the transition to the pro game).

He does not so much call 'a spade a spade' as 'a bloody big shovel', but it is this honesty that has had a huge impact on my life. I owe him a lot. Thanks Ron.

SCOTT COOKSEY (former Shrewsbury, Hereford and England non-League goalkeeper): The name Ron Jukes goes back in the Cooksey household to the 1950s as my father can remember him looking for talent on the school playing field. I first met him when I was twenty-eight and languishing in the Shrewsbury Town reserve team. I think Ron must have been desperate for a goalkeeper when he asked me to join Hereford in February 2000. No-one could have been more supportive to me. He kicked me in the appropriate place when I needed it, but always picked me up when I was down. When I was recovering from the injury that eventually ended my career, Ron rang the hospital every day. I often travelled with him to Hereford during my rehabilitation, discussing my career, his career and life in general. He also seemed to know every café, pub or restaurant en route, as he really loves his food. My one regret is that I wasn't able to play more games for Hereford in order to repay Ron's trust and confidence in my ability. I am truly grateful to Ron and Graham Turner for giving me the opportunity to play football and rediscover myself. Thanks for being there for me Ron. I shall never forget.

ARTHUR COX (former Chesterfield, Newcastle and Derby manager, assistant manager of Sunderland's 1973 FA Cup winners and England assistant manager): My first meeting with Ron was in January 1964 when he was chief scout at Walsall FC and I was invited by manager Alf Wood to join the club as first-team coach. In the last forty years, though we have worked apart for long spells, Ron and I have always remained in touch and respectful of each other.

I find it difficult to understand how Ron's wife Molly has put up with his obvious love of football all these years. He was, however, also a successful head teacher and I think his love of cricket, at which he was a good opening bat and an even better captain, was a close second to football in his sporting mistresses. This brings to mind a cricket story from a game in which I opened the innings with him in a team representing Walsall Football Club. Chasing a large total, we had passed the hundred mark when I called him for a sharp single and he was run out. That was the moment when I learned just what a fierce competitor Ron was. The glare that he gave me was such that if looks could kill I should not be here to write about Ron today. He was a very good club cricketer and very knowledgeable on the game.

Ron joined me at Derby as chief scout when he retired from teaching and the great quality that he has as a scout is that, while everyone associates Ron Jukes with schoolboy and non-League players, he has a perceptive eye too for senior League players. He does not allow a name to influence his assessment. 'Can they play in that position or can't they?' – that was the question he asked. 'Are they quick? Are they strong? What could they contribute to the club?' These were the questions he answered as he brought names forward to a manager. We were involved in the signing of players too numerous to mention.

There are a lot of footballers at all levels, past and present, who should be thankful and respect the fact that Ron Jukes knows who can play and who can't and is prepared to make his opinion known and stand by it. Long may he continue getting wet, frozen cold and everything else that goes with finding football players because, when he stops, the production line of professional football will have definitely lost a major operator.

ROBBIE DENNISON (former Wolves winger with 18 Northern Ireland caps): I first came across Ron Jukes when I was playing for West Bromwich Albion in the 1986/87 season. It was just after Steve Bull and Andy Thompson made their moves from Albion to Wolves and a friend of mine told me, after another reserve team outing, that Ron was watching again and he felt sure that I would be the next player to move to Wolves. Little did I know that I would make that move very soon. It was to be a move that changed my life, and allowed me to achieve things I had only dreamed about. I will be forever grateful for Ron's intervention.

Around that time it was Ron's football knowledge and eye for a bargain that really lifted Wolves out of the depths of despair and put them back on the footballing map. It must also be acknowledged that he helped to lay the foundations on which to build up to the achievements of today. He played his part in helping a great club make it back to the Premiership.

The people of Wolverhampton should always be grateful for the partnership of Graham Turner and Ron Jukes for their massive contribution in making this dream come true.

MICHAEL DUNFORD (former Derby County secretary and Everton chief executive): My PA Jean knocks on the door to say 'Mr Ron Jukes is on the phone; says he wants only a few seconds of your time.' Seconds turn to minutes. In fact, even hour-long conversations have become Ron's trademark. All that is a little tongue in cheek as Ron is simply a football man through and through.

He is part of Midlands football folklore. I worked with Ron when Arthur Cox invited him to work as chief scout at Derby in the 1980s. His teaching background meant that he was a stickler for detail and his professionalism is his byword. He has an eager eye for raw talent and his assessment of players over the years has, in most cases, been spot on. Hundreds of players in that period will owe a huge debt of gratitude to football's other 'Big Ron'. Always a good sounding board, Ron is eager to advise and, more importantly, he sometimes listens!

Whether you have Ron Jukes as a friend or simply a working colleague, you can truly count yourself lucky.


ALAN DURBAN (former Derby player and Shrewsbury manager with 27 Welsh caps): There's only one Ron Jukes. His reputation had gone before him long before I ever had the pleasure of meeting him. He had had successful spells at Walsall and Shrewsbury identifying talent that coaches could improve on and help to build healthy professional careers in football.

When I was Roy McFarland's assistant at Derby, Ron was introduced to me as the chief scout. He was an amicable man who loved a chortle, usually at his own joke. He was an enthusiastic cricketer, it was said, though I can't imagine him taking too many quick singles. We had some fun during that couple of years. He was always ribbed about the length of his telephone calls. Ron has earned the respect not only of those associated with the clubs he's worked for, but of the whole Midlands football fraternity. I wish him well if for no other reason than that he's a 'good bloke'.


ROB ELMES (former Halesowen, Hereford and Moor Green striker): Ron Jukes is a compulsive telephoner and a rare sleeper – he makes calls at the most ungodly hours. Ron Jukes goes for home-grown talent rather than foreign products – he chooses a steak rather than a tikka massala. Ron Jukes was a fine batsman in his day – and a first-rate teacher and head teacher. Yet it is his unquestionable talent at spotting a player that is his hallmark. It didn't stop there. Having recruited a player he has always been loyal and caring in looking after that player's interests. Ron has been the biggest influence on my career – without him I would never have managed so many games in the Conference.

MICK EVANS (former Walsall, Swansea and Crewe defender): Ron was a tremendous asset to Walsall FC during my nine years with the club. Not only did he save them hundreds of thousands of pounds in the transfer market with his astute talent-spotting ability but, in many cases, after several years' service players were sold on to help to keep the club solvent.

From a personal point of view, Ron gave me very helpful advice on strengths and weaknesses of opposition players that I had to face from his vast knowledge of teams up and down the country. His talent included his ability not only to spot future international players such as Allan Clarke and Phil Parkes, but also to spot players whom other clubs had missed but who he realised with the right coaching and fitness development could become tremendous club men. Just think of men like Nick Athey, Stan Bennett, Frank Gregg, Brian Caswell, Mark Rees and Kenny Mower, to name just a few of his signings, who played the game with determination and team spirit over many years. Many thanks, Ron, for seeing something in me. I will always be grateful to you for starting me off on a fourteen-year professional career.

TREVOR FOSTER (former Walsall striker): As one of Ron's many signings for Walsall I have many special memories of him. Twice he went the extra mile by chauffeuring me to games that I could not otherwise have played in. The first of these was when I was a late selection for Birmingham County FA in a game at Stratford-upon-Avon. Ron not only drove me there and back, but shared his sandwiches with me en route. Then, when I had been selected to make my Walsall first-team debut in a friendly game at Shrewsbury, I was unable to leave work early enough to catch the team coach. Ron picked me up as I came out of work at Tipton and drove me to the game. Ron was also captain of Blakenall Cricket Club and, hearing that I was a useful cricketer, invited me to spend what was a very enjoyable season with them.

RON GREEN (former Walsall, Shrewsbury and much-travelled goalkeeper): It was in 1977 that Ron Jukes, as Walsall chief scout, accompanied manager Dave Mackay to see me play for Alvechurch at Brereton. I was lucky enough to save a penalty and soon afterward I became a Walsall player. Firm but fair, he gave nothing away in his desire to seek nothing but the best for the club for whom he was working. Ron signed more than half the Walsall team who sensationally drew 2-2 against Liverpool at Anfield in a Milk Cup semi-final in February 1984. I was in goal on that unforgettable night.

I have bumped into him from time to time over the years since then and I can honestly say that I have never met anyone like him. Even after I had finally retired from the game at the age of forty-five, he tried to persuade me to help him meet a goalkeeping emergency at Hereford. Since then he has taken on a new challenge at Telford. Yes, there's only one Ron Jukes.

FRANK GREGG (444 games for Walsall): I was destined to work in a local foundry when I left school. Although playing for local and district schoolboy teams no-one had been in touch from a professional club. Then, one night while watching television with my parents, I heard a knock on the door. I answered it and there stood a massive figure of a man. Within minutes he had asked me to join the ground staff at Fellows Park and the rest, as they say, is history.

In short Ron Jukes was my saviour, the man who changed my life's path and I shall always be grateful to him for seeing something in me that other scouts had missed. That's why he's so special and so respected in the game.

HARRY GREGG (former Manchester United and Northern Ireland goalkeeper and Shrewsbury, Swansea and Crewe manager): I first met Ron when I was in my first managerial appointment at Shrewsbury. He was then scouting for Walsall and time and again we met up at grounds, often when we were both trying to remain unnoticed as we watched games on near-empty, off-the-map grounds. This continued during my time at Swansea and Crewe. As we chatted it became obvious that we were looking for the same qualities in players, namely genuine ability and real character. In short, Ron is a really nice person who loves and knows his football.

STEVE GRIFFITHS (Midlands scout): I first encountered Ron in the early 1990s, having taken up scouting for Hednesford Town and Crewe Alexandra after moving down to the Midlands from my native Yorkshire. It soon became apparent that here was a man who was clearly a major adversary and a significant influence in the scouting network in the area. Indeed, if any player showed promise anywhere it was virtually guaranteed that Ron would already be aware of him. It is his tenacious appetite and total commitment to the game that singles him out as someone special and anyone starting out on a scouting career could not do better than to seek his advice first. I have always valued his professional opinion on a player but now more importantly value him as a friend.

KEN GUTTRIDGE: (former Wolves, Derby and Preston scout): As I think of Ron Jukes I think of my first joint-scouting expedition – a long journey to Hartlepool on a winter's day in 1986. He stopped at a lay-by and produced sandwiches, soup and coffee. That was the thoroughness of every aspect of Ron's work. Planning with meticulous detail, always thinking ahead, always enthusiastic to go out to a game locally or hundreds of miles away if he thought there was a possible signing.

Ron has a sort of intuitive second sight when assessing the potential of a schoolboy and channels of communication to initiate and/or take further an enquiry about a player. Ron is certainly the best scout I have worked with in my many years of looking for talent. He always did a first-rate job and made no great financial demands. He has always been a credit to the game and a pleasure to work with.

GARY HACKETT (former Shrewsbury, WBA, Stoke and Aberdeen player and joint-manager of Bromsgrove and Stourbridge): Ron is not a man for small talk but every word counts when he is speaking. My first meeting with him dates back to March 1983 when he spotted me playing for Bromsgrove Rovers when he was scouting for Shrewsbury. He was already something of a scouting legend in the West Midlands and it was a great boost to my ego to be spotted by him.

I went on to have a very long and happy career in the Football League, but I shall never forget the man who started me on that path. Happily I still speak to him from time to time and his experience and knowledge of the game still shines through. Ron, you are a big man in so many ways and I feel privileged to know you.

JACK HARRIS (former Walsall and Wolves director): Ron Jukes and I have been friends for over thirty years. I first met him in the late 1960s when I joined the board at Walsall and he was chief scout. I was immediately impressed by his encyclopaedic knowledge of the game at all levels. Many of the young players signed by him progressed to the Walsall first team and no fewer than seven of them were in the team that forced a Milk Cup semi-final draw against Liverpool at Anfield in 1984.

Then, later, in the 1980s when Wolves were at their lowest ebb, Ron was the person I thought of to help manager Graham Turner build a new team. In no time at all he had recommended three Albion reserve players – Steve Bull, Andy Thompson and Robbie Dennison. At that time Ron's office at Molineux contained a bucket to catch the water coming through the roof, but Ron was an integral part of the reconstruction operation that saw Wolves winning promotion twice in successive seasons – and winning the Leyland DAF Trophy for good measure, watched by 80,000 fans, a far cry from the 3,000 gates that Wolves were attracting when Ron arrived at Molineux.

COLIN HARRISON (holder of Walsall appearance record of 529 games): I am very honoured to write about Ron Jukes, the conscientious and knowledgeable football scout who brought many local talented footballers to Walsall and other clubs. My initial meetings with Ron involved him meeting myself at my family home – and he was always afraid of the dog. While so many admired Ron for his scouting talents, I was particularly fortunate not only to be signed by him but also to work alongside him while coaching the youth team near the end of my professional career.

I say a sincere thank you to Ron for recognising my ability and giving me the chance to fulfil my ambitions as a professional footballer.

HARRY HARRISON (former club cricketer and Black Country comedian): I played with Ron at cricket on a number of occasions for Coseley Crusaders. The dedication he gave to all he did in football came out even in friendly cricket matches. He has always been a 'bostin' bloke to know and to have in your team. What's more, he was a good player.

LEON HICKMAN (freelance writer and formerly *Birmingham Post & Mail* head of sport): Sometimes I wonder whether Ron Jukes thinks he is unobtrusive; one of football's grey spies, merging into the background of bare oaks, hawthorns or cheering dads that so often fringe football fields around the country: one of Smiley's people.

He isn't. He's big, partly because he loves his grub, partly, well, because he's the best football spy in the business and everyone knows him anyway. Jukesy loves his secrets. Oh yes, he hints and he implies, but anyone who has stood on a touchline with him knows he'll only tell you what he wants, and not a drop more. When the gems do come, hang on to them, as I should have when he tipped me off first time around that Graham Taylor would be Villa manager two weeks before it actually happened. And he'll chat forever but, remember, he has the total recall of the excellent headmaster he was, and may use it years later when you have long forgotten who the player was or what he did. His personal secret is that he is utterly loyal to those he believes in, loving detail, the more arcane the better. A weighty and splendid man, Jukesy may have been an opening batsman but the cunning is all a leg-spinner's.

ALAN HILL (former Rotherham goalkeeper and Nottingham Forest youth development officer): I first met Ron in the early 1970s when I was youth development officer at Nottingham Forest. Every game that I attended at youth, non-League and senior level, this distinguished-looking, portly man also seemed to be there, speaking to parents, trainers and youth managers. He was obviously dedicated to the task of finding the next up-and-coming star, and I was curious to find out who this man was, working on my patch in the Nottingham area.

When I was eventually introduced to him, I was amazed to discover that he was a headmaster, as well as being chief scout at Walsall, later on to move to Derby and then Wolves in the same position. I found him to be a man of great integrity, with a wealth of footballing knowledge, and highly respected at all levels of the game. I am proud to consider Ron to be a friend, and appreciate all the help and advice he has shared with me over the years.

KEN HILL (former Walsall and Norwich midfielder): In the fifty-plus years that I have known Ron Jukes, two particular characteristics stand out: his enthusiasm for whatever he was doing and the note of authority in whatever he did. As a teacher at North Walsall School his bellows along corridors made even the least-disciplined pupil stop to think. As a chief scout he consistently refused to take no for an answer if there was a player he wanted.

When I played for Walsall boys I was always aware of his presence on the touchline, moving up and down like a caged tiger. Ron's determination not to be second was instilled in all who came within his charge and when I met him again recently at a players' reunion I could see that in his seventies he hadn't changed.

DICK HOMDEN (former Walsall director and Wolves chairman): I first met Ron many years ago when I became a director of Walsall FC. I found him to be extremely knowledgeable on all football matters and possessed of a natural gift for spotting a player with talent at a very early age. That gift has been underlined time and again when one looks at his signings for the clubs where he has worked, names such as Colin Harrison, David Preece, Colin Taylor and Bernie Wright.

All these were signed while he was with Walsall and I rated Ron so highly that when I joined Wolves as chairman in 1986 my first and unsurpassed signing was Ron. He in turn signed Steve Bull, Andy Thompson and Robbie Dennison, all from West Bromwich Albion, and Mark Venus from Leicester. All football clubs are the same in that the manager always gets the glory and the chairman the blame while the chief scout is never mentioned. This in no way affected Ron's commitment. He never faltered, such was his love of the game. To sum up, all the clubs that have had his services have not yet been able to replace him.

BRIAN HORTON (over 600 Football League games as a player and over 1,000 games in charge of various Football League teams as manager): Ron tells me that he first saw me playing for Cannock Schoolboys alongside David Rushbury, who went to Birmingham. In due course I joined Walsall as a teenager in the mid-1960s and Ron seemed to rate me, but I was released in 1966 without playing for the first team. Over the years I have often joked with Ron about this (though it wasn't funny at the time) and the fact that none of my 605 Football League games were for Walsall. He has readily admitted that I proved the club wrong.

In those early days I saw him as a genial, knowledgeable scout and his record over the years speaks for itself. During my managerial career I have had many conversations with him about players and their potential. His opinions are always incisive and firmly based.

Ron is one of the game's unsung heroes. Managers usually get the praise for astute signings but time and again it is men like Ron who are behind them. Ron's dedication to the game, even in his mid-seventies, is as great as ever and his judgment is as clear as ever. Long may he continue.

GEORGE HYDE (former Hereford United director, former mayor of Hereford and present Hereford city councillor): I've only known Ron for a few years, since we were both asked by Graham Turner to join the completely new board of directors at Hereford United. Although I was aware of Ron's reputation we had never met and I was immediately impressed by his open involvement in all discussions about the club's inherited problems. He has a happy knack of only saying what is relevant and asking searching questions when there might be a temptation to gloss over an item.

His contribution in terms of knowledge of footballers' ability and avail-ability is incalculable. I cannot overstate his devotion and dedication to all matters football and never cease to be amazed by the miles he travels and the number of games he watches, especially in the lower echelons of Midlands football.

A friendly, open and honest Midlander with a wicked sense of humour, it is a pleasure for him to have become a part of my life.


MICK JONES (former Peterborough, Halifax and Telford manager): A few years ago when I was with Plymouth Argyle and had made the long journey to Telford to look at a particular player, Ron Jukes insisted that there was no way I should make the long journey back on an empty stomach. He told me to follow him from the old Bucks Head in order to find 'the best fish and chips in the UK'. We ended up in Walsall and yes, they were the best fish and chips in the UK. I had always expected to find the best fish and chips in Blackpool, Southend, Scarborough or my home town Sunderland, but only Ron Jukes could have persuaded me that Walsall was the Mecca as far as fish and chips were concerned.

Not long ago I was invited to the European Cup tie between Manchester United and FC Basle. I mentioned this to Ron and in his usual gruff manner he commented, 'You won't get me to watch that rubbish.' Ron is far happier at an isolated non-League ground looking for another jewel. The list of players Ron has found is extensive and endless. I say endless because he is still producing and, ironically, worked with me at Telford United. Ron has found some great talents, usually from the unlikeliest of places such as Pelsall Villa, Rushall or Grosvenor Park, not Old Trafford. Yes – some of the best players, like the best fish and chips, have come from the environs of Walsall.

I can vividly recall our first ever conversation when I was having a great time at Huddersfield Town. I received a call from Derby County's chief scout. In what is now a very recognisable voice he said, 'Hello, I'm looking for a scout to work in the Yorkshire area. Know anyone?' 'Yes,' I replied. 'Who?' he asked. 'John Hasleden.' 'Got a number for him?' I gave Ron the number. Two months later he came back to me in typical Jukesy style. 'Hasleden, excellent, thorough, professional, precise, makes decisions, I like him.' 'Good,' I said and then, as I was putting down the receiver, Ron added, laughing, 'You didn't tell me how high his expenses would be.'

Our relationship and mutual respect started that day. Apart from the obvious words, my favourite descriptions of Ron are 'impish devilish, mischievous' and as he is on the trail of a potential signing that sparkle in his eyes is a sight to behold. At seventy-five years of age that sparkle is as bright as ever.

STAN JONES (over 500 games for Walsall and West Brom): During my two spells at Walsall I was continually impressed by the number of local lads who became professionals at Fellows Park. Ron proved again and again just what a fine breeding ground the Midlands is for football talent. Often half the first team and most of the reserve team were Ron's discoveries, the key to his success being that he concentrated on the thirteen to eighteen age group.

One final thought. After trying for years to buy success, Manchester United finally achieved it with a bunch of home-grown players, such as Beckham, Butt, Giggs, the Nevilles and Scholes – in short they did it the Ron Jukes way.

MICK KEARNS (former Oxford and Walsall goalkeeper, capped 18 times by Republic of Ireland): Ron Jukes has always had the unrelenting desire to find good players, be they at the primary school or the professional stage. To me he has always seemed to belong to the unofficial 'Crafty Scouts Association', always wanting to know whom others are looking at but never revealing whom he himself was watching.

I remember some years ago telling him about a young player I had seen in non-League football. Ron appeared to take no interest, but the next time I went to watch the lad Ron was there and a few days later I read in the newspaper that the club Ron was scouting for had snapped him up. With Ron there was always a positive assessment of a player. 'Either he can play or he can't.'

ROBERT KELLY (former Wolves player and coach and head of youth academy at Blackburn): Ron Jukes will always be a big man to me. As a naïve young coach taking his first steps in a harsh game I was in need of a guiding hand. That hand came in the form of many long trips to Scotland, hours spent in the car with football the only topic of conversation. All I had to do was sit there, listen (and drive!) while I was given the opportunity to learn from a master craftsman.

Since those Vauxhall Cavalier days I have lost count how many times Ron's voice has popped into my head, steering my course. Ron Jukes will always be a big man to me.


ROY McFARLAND (28 England caps and former Derby and Bolton manager, now manager of Chesterfield): 'Simply the best, better than all the rest.' No, not Tina Turner, but Ron Jukes. When he became chief scout of Derby County, I was assistant manager and Arthur Cox was manager. Ron gave me a wonderful insight into his scouting methods with a reputation throughout football second to none, especially in his home territory, the Midlands.

Ron loves his job with the enthusiasm of a five-year-old opening presents on Christmas Day. His phone calls at all hours of the day are legendary and are spattered with some of the worst jokes one has ever heard. Keep going Ron. You are the best.


MICHAEL McINDOE (former Hereford and Yeovil midfielder now with Doncaster): I first met Ron in June 2000. I had just been released by Luton Town and was hungry to get back into football. As a young lad I had been a bit off the rails and nobody at the time was prepared to take a chance on me as a football player because of my personal problems. 'Big Ron' saw through all that and he has an eye for the problems of young players, plucking them out of nowhere and turning them into true professionals. In my opinion 'Big Ron' is one of the best scouts in the country. To this day I will never know how he got hold of me at a friend's house in St Albans when I didn't give the number to anyone.

Joan Fennessy and Graham Turner at Hereford United deserve a lot of praise for reviving my career, but 'Big Ron' kick-started everything as a person and a player. I owed a great debt to a man who gave me a chance.

DAVE MACKAY (22 Scotland caps, former Derby, Birmingham and Walsall manager): Ron Jukes was in situ as Walsall chief scout when I took over as manager in March 1977. The team were perilously near the bottom of the Third Division at the time and Ron was one of the people I looked to as we sought to avoid relegation from the Third Division within weeks and to build a stronger team within months.

Both objectives were achieved. We lost only 2 of the last 15 games that season and in the following season we finished in sixth place and would have been in the play-offs if they had existed then. Throughout our time together Ron had an excellent working relationship with myself and my assistant manager Des Anderson and, though he had more contact with Des than with me, I came to respect his knowledge of the game, his eye for a player's ability and his integrity.

I have happy memories of joint trips out, such as the evening we watched Ron Green play for Alvechurch at Brereton. Ron was signed shortly afterwards and went on to play 265 times in goal for Walsall. Memories of other discoveries of Ron's career come floating back – Gary Shelton, who soon moved on to Aston Villa to ease Walsall's financial situation; Ian Paul, a great little defender whose career was cut short by injury; sharpshooter Don Penn, midfielder Alan Birch and others like Mark Rees who were juniors when I was with Walsall but whose careers flourished later.

I enjoyed my time at Walsall and Ron was an integral part of a brave little club into whose history his name is indelibly etched.


GAVIN MAHON (former Wolves, Hereford and Brentford midfielder now with Watford): If someone asked me to describe Ron in a single sentence I'd say Ron Jukes is the chief of all scouts. Ron has been a great part of my football career ever since I was a schoolboy at Wolves at the age of fifteen. I'm now twenty-nine and he's still about, larger than life.

I have tremendous respect for the way he's not afraid to take a gamble on non-League players. Many a scout would not give these players a look-in but this 'chief of scouts' knows exactly what to look for in a player. He never fails to put a smile on my face though he may not realise it. I love the messages he puts on my answerphone, such as 'Gav, Ron. Call me.' Football nowadays could do with a lot more people like Ron, a football man through and through. The more I've got to know Ron over the years the more I think of him not only as a great scout but a good friend too.

CHRIS MARSDEN (former Stockport, Huddersfield, Wolves, Southampton and Sheffield Wednesday midfielder): It is over ten years since I first came across Ron Jukes but the impression is still very vivid. When he rang me the conversation was not the obvious 'Do you want to play for us, son?' but a chat about all sorts of seemingly irrelevant matters. I wondered for a time whether he was working for the government in the Secret Service department. I have always enjoyed conversations with Ron though.

He has always been a fan of left footers and I think it's safe to say that if it hadn't been for Ron's perseverance (particularly after my cruciate injury) and belief in my ability, my career would not be where it is now.

PAUL MARSTON (long-serving *Birmingham Post and Mail* reporter and personal friend): During his career as a talent finder with Walsall, Shrewsbury, Birmingham, Wolves, Derby, Hereford and Telford I dubbed Ron Jukes 'Super Scout'. It was no exaggeration. He always had that special ability to attend a match – more often than not non-League – and discover a little diamond who would go on to make an excellent career in professional soccer. And there were times when he would pinch a player from right under the noses of rival scouts sent to watch someone else.

'Jukesy' used anyone he could to sniff out a star. Usually when I returned home from covering a Walsall match he would ring me and ask if anyone in the opposition side had impressed me. Sometimes I named the very man he was interested in, but on other occasions my nomination received the curt response 'He can't play for s★★★.' I remember telling him a new Walsall player had done extremely well on his debut – good pace, neat skill and an ability to deliver good corners. Having listened patiently to my enthusiastic appraisal, Jukesy snapped: 'He's got a heart like a pea.' I argued with him about that one, and he said, 'Okay, I will ring you after he has made six appearances for Walsall and get your reaction.' True to his word, he rang after the player's sixth match and asked what I thought. 'Heart like a pea,' I admitted.

Ron first made his name with the Saddlers and, during his long career at Fellows Park as a part-time scout, the club was usually strapped for cash, so he had to find bargains who would cost next to nothing but were frequently sold for a bumper profit. Allan 'Sniffer' Clarke and goalkeeper Phil Parkes (both England internationals) were just two in that category. That style of business kept the Cinderella club alive.

There were even times when the Saddlers could send out a team with up to NINE players that he had found in the Midlands. The men that he took to the club could be guaranteed to give 100 per cent, men like Nick Atthey, Stan Bennett, Alan Boswell, Frank Gregg, Colin Harrison, David Preece, Mark Rees and Colin Taylor.

Jukesy never missed a trick. I remember when he was Wolves' chief scout and they were beginning their Steve Bull-inspired revival. He told me after one match at Molineux I attended that they needed a new goalkeeper. The following day I bought the Sunday papers, but played golf and didn't start reading them until I went to bed early that evening. I spotted a short *Sunday Express* report on a Newport County match in which there was a mention of another goalkeeper, not Mark Kendall. I had seen Kendall in the Newport side against Walsall a few weeks earlier, so I wondered why he was not in the side. Was he injured, or dropped or what? So I picked up the bedside phone, told Ron what I had seen, and his brief response was 'I'll think about it.' A few days later I picked up the local evening papers and the back page banner headlines screamed 'Kendall Joins Wolves'. Jukesy had got his man, once again.

During my newspaper career I became friendly with many of Jukesy's discoveries, and they always spoke very highly of the headmaster's knowledge of the game and of his persuasive ability. A disciplinarian in his teaching career, he usually looked for, and found, players who had discipline in their game. Whichever club he worked for, big Ron left behind a rich legacy of talented players. His secret? Hard work, and the fact that he knew 'who could play'.

GEOFF MORRIS (former Walsall, Shrewsbury and Port Vale winger): I am honoured to be asked for my recollections of Ron Jukes, particularly the illustrious company I am in. I first met 'Jukesy' when I was a chronically asthmatic fourteen-year-old schoolboy who couldn't run fifty yards without wheezing and coughing. Not a good sign for a prospective professional footballer, but that was my ambition.

Being born and bred in West Bromwich and a fanatical Albion fan, I was delighted when they declared an interest in me but, on receiving a specialist medical report, they released me. This being the background, I was at a very low ebb in my life. Football was everything to me but it seemed that my health was going to stand in the way of me reaching my full potential. Ron was chief scout at Walsall at this time and said he wanted a five-minute chat with me and my parents. We actually talked for about two hours but in that time he changed my life. He didn't talk about football that much but he talked about people who had overcome problems in life and had gone on to achieve their ambitions.

I remember Ron as a jovial, immensely compassionate man. I hope thoughts of the Saddlers' victory over Villa and the two goals I scored keep us both warm on cold winter nights and in some way repay the enormous debt I owe him for encouraging me to follow my dream.


KENNY MOWER (484 games for Walsall): When I was fourteen and playing for a junior club my team manager of that time told my teammates and myself that there was a scout from a professional club coming to watch us play. Every time the ball went out of play I scoured the touchline for a sight of this scout, but I could see only parents. Then late in the game I heard a bellow from the touchline, 'Pass the ball.' I looked up and saw a large man in a sheepskin coat.

I then saw the stranger walking away and after the game I learned from my team manager that the man in the sheepskin coat had been the scout. I thought I had missed my chance, but about a year later Ron Jukes arrived to watch another of my team's games. This time he stayed to the end and approached me to see if I was interested in going for trials with Walsall FC. Things developed from there. I signed apprenticeship forms with Walsall and from time to time saw Ron at games. He would often shout a few words of encouragement and then disappear. It was only later that I learned of all the players he had discovered. What a man and what a scout.

CHRIS MURPHY (Shrewsbury, Telford and Cheltenham striker): I first met Ron in the summer of 2003 after I had been released by Shrewsbury Town. He phoned me and asked to meet my father and I. I found him to be a man of few words but every word mattered. Not only did he offer me a chance at Telford United, but he kept to his word and I began the happiest and most successful part of my career to date.

Ron's knowledge of the game and of those connected with it is quite remarkable. His brain quickly kicks into gear and he has been a great encouragement to me. He was quickly on the phone to congratulate me on my hat-trick against Leigh RMI. Ron is a great scout with the human touch.

TONY PAINTER (former Wolves scout, now with Blackburn Rovers): I spent ten years with Ron, most of them when he and Graham Turner were at Wolves. During those ten years I would like to think that Ron taught me an awful lot about football but also a lot about himself.

I had the impression at times that Ron treated me like the son he never had. I learned a lot from him. He was honest, but clever at times (devious in a nice sort of way). It was an education to have been part of his scouting system.

I used to love to be in the same car as him going off to matches because he always had a good story to tell that kept me interested. He was full of information and he was very loyal to the manager he worked for.

DON PEACOCK (former Blakenall cricketer and Walsall rugby player): It was in the mid-1950s that I first met E.R.P. (Ron) Jukes playing cricket for Blakenall. He had previously played for Walsall seconds in the Birmingham League and he took over as captain of Blakenall Sunday team in 1955 and of the club itself in 1956, a position he held with distinction for many years. The team contained a number of footballers, pro and semi-pro, so that at times I felt they might have put on a better performance at football than at cricket.

Be that as it may, during Ron's period as captain Blakenall enjoyed probably the most successful spell in their history thanks to his skill as an opening batsman and meticulous planning both on and off the field. His regular minute alterations to field placings and batting orders together with the rolling of wickets and tea rotas were all typical of the man. He would even have a toilet roll among his cricket gear. Off the field he owned a brand-new BSA 500cc motorbike and cut a dash at the Saturday night dance at the town hall. My friendship with Ron and his wife Molly has endured some forty-eight years and it has been both a pleasure and a privilege throughout.

KEITH PEARSON (former Wolves and Derby County secretary): I first encountered Ron in 1986 in my capacity as secretary and accountant of Wolverhampton Wanderers Football Club, when he joined the club as chief scout along with the manager Graham Turner. That was the start of a friendship that has continued right up to date although we have both moved clubs. I still speak regularly to him on the phone and continue to prepare his tax returns for him.

A man of vast experience and one with a tremendous knowledge of the game, Ron is truly respected by all associated with football. Among the many players he has brought into the game, my memories are of Steve Bull and Andy Thompson, whom he brought to Wolves from West Brom. Bully was to become Wolves' most famous striker and Thommo a well-respected defender.

Ron is a truly dedicated man who, during his forty-five years in football has earned the reputation of being a truly honest and trustworthy man at all levels of the game. Even a triple heart bypass operation did not deter him; he was soon back in the groove finding football talent for his clubs. It has been a pleasure to have worked with you Ron and still to share your friendship. Best wishes for the future.

NIGEL PEARSON (former Shrewsbury, Middlesbrough and Sheffield Wednesday defender and currently West Brom assistant manager): My first meeting with Ron Jukes was when I was at college in Nottingham and playing non-League football for Heanor Town. I played a trial game for Shrewsbury reserves at Chester. I was aware that Shrewsbury and

Chesterfield were both showing an interest in me but it was Ron on behalf of Shrewsbury who actually invited me to play in a game.

Ron came into the dressing room after the game and, as I had not previously met him, I was quite taken aback by his opening words: 'You did alright son, but you'll need to lose some weight.' I looked at him and thought 'a bit rich coming from you', and I saw Graham Turner, who was with him, having a smile to himself. This abrupt manner is, of course, an essential part of Ron and it was obvious that Ron and Graham had a tremendous trust and respect for each other's opinions.

Just one game later (a Saturday morning game for the Shrewsbury youth team) I was invited to join Shrewsbury and though I didn't meet Ron again for a while I was very happy to realise just how completely Graham had trusted Ron's judgment and gone ahead and signed me.

I've had periodic chats with Ron over the years and take it as a great compliment when he seeks my views on footballing matters. It is comforting to know that one has the respect of a man who has seen so much football and travelled so many miles in pursuit of players.

For a player, especially one taken from non-League, there is always a special bond between yourself and the person responsible for giving you the opportunity to play League football. Ron, although in the background, has had a profound effect on my career and commands my wholehearted respect, both as a man and as a professional doing his job conscientiously. I would like publicly to take the opportunity of thanking the man responsible for giving me the chance to realise every boy's dream of playing League football. Cheers Ron.


GARY PENDREY (former Birmingham player and manager, former Walsall, Wolves, Coventry and Southampton assistant manager): A man for all men or a scout for all scouts? How would you describe a scout like Ron Jukes? Selective, opinionated, mischievous, secretive, sensitive, hardworking, loyal – these are just a few of the words that come to mind. In my opinion, Ron has proved his ability through the number of players he has spotted who have had successful professional careers, some of them at the very highest level. Added to that, a pleasanter and more polite man one could not wish to meet.

DAVE PENNEY (former Derby, Oxford, Swansea and Cardiff player, now manager of Doncaster): I first met Ron in September 1985 when I was a bricklayer from Yorkshire. I was young and raw, but Ron saw something in me. He was the one who gave me the opportunity to do something I had always dreamed of, that of being a professional footballer.

As people come and go in football Ron and I moved on, though our paths would cross every now and then. Now that I am in management and Ron is still scouting in the Midlands our paths have crossed even more in the last few years. We speak at least once a week about this player, that player and everything to do with football, the game we both love.

I have a lot to thank Ron for. He was the one who gave me a chance and hopefully I have repaid the belief he had in me. Thanks Ron.

DAVID PREECE (former Walsall, Luton, Derby and Cambridge midfielder and Torquay and Telford coach): I first met Ron Jukes in 1977 when I was fourteen years old, playing for Bridgnorth Colts. He introduced himself to my parents and I after watching a game and asked if I would be interested in training at Fellows Park. He explained that he was a scout for Walsall FC and was impressed with my game. After discussions with my parents and Mr Jukes I agreed to train at Fellows Park and continue to play for the Colts and my county side, Shropshire.

Mr Jukes followed my progress closely during the next two years, even helping with lifts, as my parents didn't drive. I signed for Walsall as a professional in 1980 and from there, in 1984, I played for Luton Town. I stayed at Luton for ten years until I left for Derby County and Cambridge United. In 2001 I became player-coach at Torquay United where I kept in contact with Ron about players coming up through the divisions.

I have now known Ron for twenty-five years and he has always been supportive and encouraging throughout my career. He has a great understanding of the game and I always appreciate his thoughts and opinions.

ROBERT PURDIE (Hereford United striker): I first met Ron when I was at a crossroads after being released by Leicester City. I was immediately impressed by his straight talking and the more I got to know him the more I realised he was a man of his word. Ron was instrumental in getting

Graham Turner to review the terms offered and to sign me for Hereford
United, and in the early days showed great concern that I should settle in
there. He has kept in regular contact since then and I have always valued
his advice. If it were not for Ron Jukes I should not be where I am today,
playing for a top Conference side battling for a Football League place.


MARK RANKINE (former Doncaster, Wolves and Preston midfielder):
I first met Ron in 1992. He was instrumental in me fulfilling my football
ambitions. I was at Doncaster Rovers going nowhere when he spotted me
playing at Walsall and took me to Wolves, where I had a fantastic time.

One is instantly drawn to Mr Jukes. He is one of the most genuine
men I have met in football. His knowledge is thorough, his humour is
sometimes good but most of all he is a gentleman.


MARK REES (former Walsall winger whose pace frightened Liverpool
at Anfield in 1984): The name of Ron Jukes conjures up a picture of a
rotund figure in a brown tweedy suit and windswept hairdo stood on
the touchline of a very windy pitch, but what a eye for up-and-coming
talent.

I was one of the players Ron brought in as teenagers at Walsall in the
late 1970s, Ian Paul, Don Penn, Craig Shakespeare and David Preece being
among the others. Despite competition from all the big Midlands clubs
Ron seemed always to get the talent that he wanted. Scouts would come
along and ask Ron 'Have you seen young so-and-so play?' Immediately
Ron would respond 'Yes, I've seen him,' and then proceed to state clearly
whether he thought the player would make the grade or not. To me, Ron
was the scout who made the Walsall team who reached the Milk Cup
semi-final of 1984.


BRUCE RIOCH (24 Scotland caps, former Millwall, Bolton, Arsenal and
Norwich manager): Ron is a legend in his own lifetime. I have met him
at so many grounds, from Premier League to a variety of non-League
grounds. I shall always remember when I came back from America in the

mid-1970s and Ron, as chief scout of Derby County, asked me to cover an Oxford United game, but declined to tell me which players he was interested in so that he would have my unbiased views on who were the players worth pursuing.

Always friendly, always hospitable, Ron has always been an inspiration to talk to before and after games and whenever one met him in a club's guest room his encyclopaedic knowledge of the game was such that one always went away better informed.

ALLY ROBERTSON (former West Bromwich Albion and Wolves defender): I have rarely known anyone so positive as Ron. Whatever the situation at a club he has always been upbeat, looking forward to the next match. I have never known anyone with such an informed knowledge of players both famous and unknown. During my brief sortie into the world of management I rang Ron several times to enquire about players and he always came up with a concise assessment of strengths and/or weaknesses, even those I had not expected him to have heard of.

As a player at Wolves in the late 1980s I only wish I had had more chance of talking to him as he held balanced opinions on anything and everything, inside the game and out. Few scouts past or present can have seen so many games as Ron – he seemed to be out every night of the week and watching two or more games every Saturday and then out again on Sundays, whether at Football League grounds or on parks pitches. It is almost an understatement to say that there has only ever been one Ron Jukes.

COLIN ROBINSON (former Shrewsbury, Birmingham and Hereford player): I was playing for Mile Oak Rovers in the Midland Combination, thinking that at twenty-two I had missed the boat as far as becoming a Football League player was concerned. It was Ron Jukes who persuaded me to have a trial for Shrewsbury Town, who were at that time in the old Second Division.

All through the negotiations Ron was always there to help with any problems or questions I had and he consistently assured me that I was making the right decision. I am so glad he did as this led to ten great years as a professional footballer.

JOHN RUDGE (former much-travelled striker and Port Vale manager, current Stoke director of football): Being a Wolverhampton-born lad myself I have known Ron for many years. He is the ultimate football talent spotter and has been in the game for a long time. I have on several occasions in my career sought his advice and opinion – usually when he rings at nine o'clock in the morning.

I recall sitting next to him discussing the potential of a very green Steve Bull. While I was contemplating the situation Ron was signing the player and the rest, as they say, is history. Ron is a legend who has the uncanny ability to unearth raw talent. He is enthusiastic, dedicated and keeps on going – just like the Morris Minor. They certainly don't make them like him anymore!

CRAIG SHAKESPEARE (former Walsall and West Brom midfielder, now West Brom youth coach): When Aston Villa released me as an under-16 Ron was knocking at our front door the next day to invite me down to Walsall. That set me on the way to a career in the game.

Ron was always on the ball and had his ear to the ground getting information from all kinds of sources – he would have made a great spy. He seemed at times to be at every game played, watching five or six games a day when possible. His eye for a player is second to none and whenever I've been looking at a player he has been the first person whose opinion I've sought.

ANDY SHAW (former Telford United chairman): When I heard that Ron had left Hereford in the summer of 2003 I went straight in for him. He has all the connections and experience that one could possibly want. During his time at Telford he did us proud. He was conscientious, hard-working and set to with a will to do the job in hand. In next to no time we had a playing staff of twenty at Telford – and Ron was responsible

for eighty per cent of them. He was very supportive to me during my
time as chairman.


GARY SHELTON (650 Football League games and currently West
Bromwich Albion reserve team manager): My first recollection of Ron was
when I was playing junior football on the Embankment in Nottingham
on Saturday mornings. I remember a big man standing at a distance
watching the game and taking notes. Little did I know he was a scout
for Walsall Football Club. He became a regular feature at many games in
which I played. He finally introduced himself to my father and myself,
inviting me to train with Walsall Football Club. That was the start of my
long football career.

 Ron is a perfect gentleman and his ability for spotting football talent
is second to none. Long may it continue.


PETER SHIRTLIFF (former Sheffield Wednesday, Charlton and Wolves
defender): I was tucked up in bed at about 11 p.m. one night when the
phone rang. Confused and startled, I answered full of trepidation. It was
Ron, enquiring about a player he could possibly sign for Hereford United
and thought I might know of him. This totally sums up his dedication
to scouting and to football in general. He simply loves football. We have
had many a conversation since and I very much appreciate the advice and
knowledge he has shared with me.


JOHN SNAPE (former West Bromwich Albion, Halesowen, Hereford
and Worcester midfielder): As far as I am concerned Ron Jukes is a first-
rate football scout – and much more. Not only did he see some merit in
me as a player, he made me a better person. He taught me to respect the
higher values of truth, integrity and compassion.

 Though I was a part-time player he treated me as a full-timer. Whenever
he watched me play I felt that he was with me, heading or kicking every
ball. Yes, Ron has made me a better person and I owe him a debt I can
never repay.

MAL STARKEY (former Shrewsbury Town player and secretary, now a director): On the surface inscrutable and demanding, Ron Jukes is a most sensitive and astute scout who keeps everything close to his chest and never divulges anything that he doesn't wish to. This makes him a most competent and capable practitioner who has spotted players too numerous to calculate in their formative years and coached them to become first-rate professionals.

Suffice to say that he has few equals. I have known him for many years and worked closely with him during his time at Shrewsbury. His list of acquaintances in the game reads like a 'who's who'. In a nutshell he epitomises the professional football scout. For many years he has been one of the best in the game.

MIKE STOWELL (448 games in Wolves' goal, a club record): My most lasting memory of Ron Jukes is of a late-evening telephone call in the summer of 1990 when I was asked the most searching questions about my future plans by a voice that I did not recognise. It could have been the FBI, such was the searching nature of the questions, but actually it was Ron Jukes, seeking to take me back to Wolves after a spell on loan over a year earlier.

In due course I signed and played 441 more games for Wolves, getting to know Ron well. What a smashing chap he turned out to be, with an encyclopaedic knowledge of the game and second to none in his ability to spot talent in a player. It was good to hear that in the year of 2003 he had taken on a new challenge at Telford United, with his eyes and brain, the tools of his trade, as sharp as ever.

COLIN TAYLOR (189 goals for Walsall): It was on a tragic evening, Thursday 6 February 1958, the day of the Manchester United plane crash at Munich. A message reached me while I was looking round a record shop that I was required at home. Two men awaited me there, namely Walsall manager Bill Moore and chief scout Ron Jukes, who looked very much like the schoolteacher he was, stern and smartly dressed in a blazer.

Soon I had signed some forms and together with my Stourbridge teammate I was on Walsall's books. Soon I was earning wages I had never dreamed of up to then (£9 in the season and £7 in the summer). How grateful I was to Ron for seeing something in me that at the time I didn't realise was there. I remember travelling to training, usually with Jimmy Cochrane, the former Birmingham player who came from the same area. Soon another local lad, Frank Gregg, joined us at Fellows Park.

Twice Walsall sold me when hard up and twice bought me back when things were a little easier. So many happy memories — and all leading from that first encounter with Ron Jukes on that February evening in 1958.

PAUL TROLLOPE (former Torquay, Derby and Fulham midfielder, 4 Wales caps): I first met Ron when he was instrumental in my move from Torquay United to Derby County in 1994. Without Ron and the then Derby manager Roy McFarland I should not have enjoyed the career that I have had. His old office at the Baseball Ground seemed to be filled with football knowledge and his very presence oozed with enthusiasm. I received so many words of wisdom from our chats together.

Though both of us left Derby County in due course we have continued to speak regularly on the telephone, his unique manner and deep Midlands accent meaning that there has never been any need for formal greetings.

On a serious note, Ron has been someone I've turned to for valuable advice on any football matter, particularly possible transfers, his contacts in the game and knowledge of clubs being second to none. I shall always consider Ron to be one of my football mentors and I'm sure many others will who have worked with him over the years.

DR BILL TWEDDLE (former Wolves club doctor): It is an understatement to say that Ron Jukes is an extremely efficient scout. During his time with Wolves he was instrumental in their dramatic rise from the old Fourth Division to the top half of the old Second Division. His part in the signing of players such as Steve Bull, Andy Thompson and Robbie Dennison is well documented. What's more, Ron is a grand person to work with, popular with everyone with whom he comes in contact.

MARK VENUS (over 500 games for Hartlepool, Leicester, Wolves and Ipswich): Ron is a larger-than-life figure who lives for the game of football. I first met him fifteen years ago when as chief scout for Wolves he set up my move from Leicester City. Happily he is still very much in the game in his mid-seventies. I have kept in touch with Ron over the years because he is a genuine football friend. He pulls no punches with his opinions and many are the times that I have phoned to seek his advice.

JAMES WALL (former Derby, now Hereford defender): After being released by Derby County I attended the Lilleshall trials and though I heard that Notts County and QPR were interested in me it was Ron Jukes who was the first to contact me with an 8 a.m. phone call. As a result I signed for Hereford. It was something of a culture shock there but Ron was one of the people who made me feel welcome. His passion for the game is almost frightening. He keeps up links with his signings past and present over the years, always talking sound football sense. In a word Ron is a grand bloke and a credit to the game.

ROY WHALLEY (Walsall FC chief executive): I remember attending a Birmingham League reserve-team match in 1958 at Fellows Park, which attracted a crowd of over 4,000. Interest in this game focused on two new signings, Peter Jeavons and Colin Taylor, from Stourbridge FC, making their debuts for Walsall. While Jeavons did not make the grade, Colin Taylor went on to become a Walsall legend. He was introduced to the club by chief scout Ron Jukes, surely the greatest finder of soccer talent ever employed by Walsall FC.

Working closely with manager Bill Moore, Ron Jukes must take a lot of the credit for the success enjoyed by the club in the late 1950s and early 1960s. The Walsall youth team in the 1962/63 season included seven players, Dave Tennant, Colin Harrison, Stan Bennett, Nicky Atthey, Roger Smith, Mick Mason and Allan Clarke, all discovered by Ron Jukes, who went on to play in the Football League and, in Clarke's case, international football. An incredible feat!

The ability of Ron Jukes to spot soccer talent is unsurpassed. Although he went on to demonstrate his skills with other clubs, I will always associate him with the Saddlers and his great discoveries over a period of a quarter of a century who became favourites with the Fellows Park crowd.

IAN WILLARS (former *Birmingham Post and Mail* sports reporter): In the days before soccer academies, Ron Jukes belonged to the respected band of chief scouts appointed by Football League clubs to unearth talented young players. It was a cut-throat business with chief scouts only surviving if they delivered the goods.

In the West Midlands Ron has long been renowned for having the best eye for finding young players likely to succeed at a higher level. The word went out that if clubs were looking for players they should contact the headmaster from Walsall. The flow of players that Ron has spotted for a variety of clubs has never slowed down in nearly half a century and managers have also used him when wanting the low-down on players to look out for among the opposition in future games.

Steve Bull of Wolves and England fame, with over 300 goals to his credit, is just one of Ron's signings. Countless others have been spotted by him and gone on to successful careers in the game.

BERT WILLIAMS (former Walsall and Wolves goalkeeper, 24 England caps): My links with Ron Jukes stretch back some sixty years, though I was unaware at the time of the first of these. It was in the 1940s that Ron, then a schoolboy, watched me playing for Walsall and was one of the fine band of supporters who cheered my efforts to keep the Hillary Street and Laundry End goals intact.

Ron has told me in more recent times that he continued to be a fan of mine in my Wolves and England days, but it was in the 1960s that I first met him. I was running a goalkeeping school in Bilston at the time and Ron, in his role as Walsall chief scout, would come along and talk over the potential of young goalkeepers who were in the school and would send others in whom he saw potential for further training.

His deep knowledge of the game and absolute honesty shone through all our conversations then and he was just the same Ron when, as chief scout of Wolves in the late 1980s and early 1990s, he would invite me for a cup of coffee in his office. We talked for hours on a range of topics inside and outside football and again the depth of his perceptions and his wry sense of humour made these occasions ones I shall never forget.

JOHN WOODCOCK (former Mesty Croft School pupil): The highlight of my primary school days was playing right half in the Mesty Croft team in 1961/62 when Ron Jukes was deputy head there and in charge of football. I am just one of many people in the West Midlands for whom the word 'Jukesy' is synonymous with discipline and respect. He treated his school football team like professionals, demanding the same high standards. I still glow with pride when I remember someone telling me that Ron had said 'Woodcock wasn't a good footballer, but when he lost the ball he always went and tackled back.'

I am now a school governor and when I hear school sports being discussed I think of the high standards Ron set in running such events. It was Ron who taught me to swim at the age of ten – and I have been swimming a mile a day for over thirteen years. Ron taught me how to draw in perspective and architectural drawings now represent a large section of my professional work.

BERNIE WRIGHT (scorer of the opening goal in Walsall's 3-2 FA Cup win over Manchester United in January 1975): After being badly let down by broken promises from other chief scouts, I was very suspicious when Ron Jukes introduced himself to me after I had written to Walsall FC requesting a trial. I was quite aggressive towards him, but over a period of time I began to trust him and he proved himself to be worthy of that trust and a man of integrity.

I did eventually sign for Walsall and we became good friends. When I returned to Walsall from Everton he was the first person from Walsall that I met. He showed a lot of patience and was always ready to help myself and any other player who had problems. In my twenties I was somewhat wild and it could not have been easy for him. Thanks Ron for all your help.

IAN WRIGHT (former Bristol Rovers and Hull now Hereford defender): The first time that I spoke to Ron was on the phone when he was trying to sign me for Hereford United. There are two things you can say about Ron and these are that he is persistent and determined. From the first time we spoke to the time I signed, which was about three weeks later, he was constantly on the phone. He would ask me my thoughts, wonder what I was going to do and whether there was anything he could do to help me.

I have known Ron for five years and throughout this time he would ring me regularly about all sorts of football-related matters. He was always concerned about what he called 'his players'. He would like to know how any new players were settling in and what the atmosphere was like in the dressing room. If trialists or new players were coming he would ring me to make sure that I knew a little about them, their playing history and, more than anything, to make sure that I made an effort to ensure that they felt welcome at the club. These things were very important to him.

Ron is a thoughtful and concerned person who takes his interest in football very seriously. He thinks about all avenues of football and is indeed very knowledgeable and has a thorough experience of the game. He made me feel important to my club and for this he will always have my respect.

# RON SAYS ABOUT THEM

COLIN ADDISON: I regularly met him on scouting missions when he was coaching and managing in the Football League. On such occasions he and I frequently swapped ideas and I found him to be a fine raconteur. We have had many telephone conversations over the years and in recent times I have met him during his days as manager first of Yeovil and then of Forest Green in the Conference.

GRAHAM ALLNER: I first met Graham as a promising left winger in Birmingham junior football. Though he claims that I signed him for Walsall after a bad game I had in fact seen him on several occasions and realised that he had good pace, two good feet, the ability to score goals and a football brain. Though he never made it into League football he played for several Midlands non-League clubs and has since managed AP Leamington, Kidderminster and Cheltenham. Those who have played for him speak highly of his character and spectators testify that his teams have always played good football. He is, at the time of writing, with Aston Villa.

RON ATKINSON: As a player he had what I felt were the ingredients of a perfect skipper. As captain of Headington before and after they changed their name to Oxford, Ron was what I regarded as a traffic controller on the field, the sort of player I should like to have been myself, worth his place for his captaincy quite apart from his other contributions to a game. His influence on individuals and teams has been immense and while most people associate him with West Bromwich Albion, Aston Villa and Manchester United, I think also of his earlier successful spells at Kettering and Cambridge when he was cutting his managerial teeth.

NICK ATTHEY: One of my first batch of young players to sign for Walsall, Nick hailed from the North-East, but I found him playing for Coventry Schools and signed him as a schoolboy at fifteen. He left eighteen years and 502 games later. He is the perfect example of the bread-and-butter player who never gives less than his best. He settled in Aldridge near Walsall after marrying the daughter of former Football League referee Arthur Rowbotham and still keeps in close touch with me.

CHIC BATES: He was a prolific goalscorer alongside Ray Hayward in his Stourbridge days and at that time I tried unsuccessfully to sign him for Walsall. Later I linked up with him again when he was first coach and then manager of Shrewsbury. He is still going strong in 2004 as coach at Shrewsbury.

STAN BENNETT: I first saw Stan as a young, blond centre half captaining Aston boys. I took him to Walsall where he became one of their most popular players ever. He played 438 games for his one and only League club and many felt that he was released too soon. His success gave me a great deal of pleasure. Now living in the Cirencester area, he recommended a footballing kick-boxer to me when I was with Wolves.

DAVID BROWN: I knew David's family well and at school he was a sports fanatic. I spent many hours with him and others in the school playground after school and I didn't realise that I was coaching a future England opening bowler. Later I opened the innings for Blakenall when he was opening the bowling for Walsall. He was genuinely fast, bringing the ball down from a great height and I had bruises to prove it, though he rarely got me out. At least that's my story. He was a wonderful ambassador for his county and country. I must confess, though, that I had no influence on his later career as a racehorse man.

ALAN BUCKLEY: Walsall's record goalscorer with 205 goals in 483 games, Alan scored a hat-trick on his home debut for Walsall in 1973 and despite his lack of inches he had a splendid touch in either foot. During his time as Walsall manager many claimed that they played the best football in the history of the club. Since his move from Walsall in 1996 he and I have regularly swapped information on players. We are both proud owners of golden retrievers. Alan was a goalscoring legend.

BRIAN CASWELL: Metaphorically speaking I have known Brian from the cradle to middle age. At Mesty Croft School he was in the school football team as a goalkeeper at the age of seven, but soon he was showing ability as an outfield player both in defence and attack. He also played cricket, ran, jumped and swam for the school. I always thought he was destined for League football and he went on to play 458 games for Walsall, and then to have spells with Doncaster, Leeds and Wolves. He later became an FA coach and worked for a variety of clubs including Birmingham, Northampton, Shrewsbury and Telford.

ALLAN CLARKE: The second of a family of five boys who all played League football. He showed outstanding talent in his days with South-East Staffs Schoolboys and I signed him for Walsall in the midst of fierce competition from other clubs. A quiet lad who exploded on the football field, Allan was, I felt, sold cheaply by Walsall to Fulham from where he went on to Leicester and Leeds, scoring 10 goals for England. After scoring goals at all levels of the game he managed Barnsley, Leeds, Lincoln and Scunthorpe and I was delighted when, in 1998, he accepted the invitation to my seventieth birthday and drove down from Scunthorpe to the Midlands to be there.

BILL CLAYTON: A football fanatic who would watch a game 365 days a year, Bill gave yeoman service as a scout to Wolves, Derby, Hereford and Preston.

ARTHUR COX: The consummate professional even in his early days at Walsall after his playing career had been ended by injury while still in his teens. He lived with me for a short time during his Walsall days after a family bereavement. A tremendous competitor, Arthur took as much pleasure in the reserves winning as the first team. Beneath his brusque exterior he has a heart of gold, thoughtful and caring in his dealing with players. He gave me my first full-time post in football as chief scout of Derby County when he was manager there. His instructions to me when he wanted a particular player watched were short and to the point: 'Watch him. I want an answer.' He announced his retirement in 2004 after serving with Kevin Keegan in his Fulham, England and Manchester City days, but I doubt whether the game has seen the last of him. A devoted family man, Arthur is a most proficient gardener now living near Burton upon Trent. Arthur both gives and earns respect and has always been utterly reliable and dependable.

ROBBIE DENNISON: A delightfully thoughtful and respectful Irishman who was nearly as good a cricketer as footballer. A deadly taker of free-kicks, Robbie spent nearly a decade with Wolves and gave tremendous service.

MICHAEL DUNFORD: Michael must be regarded as one of the best administrators in the game. I first met him at Derby where in twenty-four hours he told me everything about the club. He earned the respect of all in the game for his efficiency and co-operation. I was surprised when he moved from Derby to Everton, as he was a Derby County fan to the core.

ALAN DURBAN: A bubbly, fast-talking Welshman. A fine inside forward in his Derby days, I knew him first as manager of Shrewsbury and later as coach at Derby. He was another person with whom it was a delight to work.

ROB ELMES: A schoolteacher who made the transition from playing part-time at Halesowen to playing among mainly full-time players at Hereford. Possessed of excellent aerial ability, Rob scored some fine goals during his two seasons at Hereford.

MICK EVANS: A powerful defender with a fine left foot, Mick was signed by me for Walsall from Vono Sports. He later played under Harry Gregg's management at Swansea and Crewe and then, after spells with several non-League clubs, he played in charity games into his fifties. In 2004 he was scouting for me at Telford.

TREVOR FOSTER: One of the few players I signed after he wrote in for a trial, Trevor came to Walsall from the Joseph Leckie School, scoring a hat-trick in a trial game in Pleck Park and revealing a body swerve second to none. Much was expected of Trevor, but he dropped out of League football after just 63 games. He did, however, look to the future by studying diligently in his spare time.

RON GREEN: The circumstances of this signing are described in detail in the opening chapter of this book. He was in his mid-forties when he finally hung up his boots in 2003. He played in several 'big' games for Walsall, where he spent his best days.

KEN GUTTRIDGE: Ken has been a long-time loyal and supportive colleague with whom I have travelled many miles and talked about many players. I have always had the utmost respect for his opinions.

GARY HACKETT: Gary was one of my first signings for Shrewsbury when he came from Bromsgrove. A skilful, fleet-footed winger with two good feet, Gary went on to a career with Stoke, West Brom and Motherwell and at the time of writing is joint manager of Stourbridge.

JACK HARRIS: As a director, first at Walsall and later at Wolves, Jack showed unfailing loyalty and devotion to the club he was working for. He and Dick Homden were inseparable for many years and to me the breakdown of their relationship while at Wolves was a tragedy. It is a breach that I would dearly like to have healed, but sadly Jack died in 2005.

COLIN HARRISON: The ideal utility man, Colin played a record 530 games for Walsall, his one and only Football League club. Quiet and shy off the field, he was a keen competitor on it.

LEON HICKMAN: One of the old school of soccer journalists. After many years with the *Birmingham Evening Mail* he has been freelance for the last few years and I was delighted when this very knowledgeable scribe agreed to contribute to this book. He has a strong individual style of writing and I always look forward to reading what he has to say on any burning issue.

ALAN HILL: A former goalkeeper who for a time was a rival scout. He and I soon became close friends, however, and we have helped each other many times.

KENNY HILL: Like Brian Caswell he was both taught by me at school and played for Walsall while I was chief scout there. He is the perfect example of the honest, hard-working midfielder.

DICK HOMDEN: A Shropshire lad like Jack Harris, Dick is a keen football fan with whom I worked at both Walsall and Wolves, though he always maintained his affection for his home-town club Shrewsbury. As a director he made a great contribution to both Walsall and Wolves and brought an enthusiasm to both boardrooms. We have kept in touch through the years.

BRIAN HORTON: A Cannock schoolboy who was signed by me for Walsall, but who went on to play over 600 games for other League clubs and has since made his way in management. He is mentioned elsewhere in this book as someone I have regarded as the ideal captain. He always led from the front and 'conducted' his team. He always seemed to me to be the spark that set his team alight. He was the manager's voice on the field and he always seemed to have the respect of his team. What a competitor! Always in the thick of things.

STAN JONES: An outstanding central defender, powerful in the air. He was with Walsall when I first joined them in 1957/58. He regularly visited Molly and I when he came home on leave from National Service and sometimes stayed for a bite to eat before games. In later years he played cricket with me at Blakenall. He had eight successful years with West Bromwich Albion in between his two spells at Walsall.

ROBERT KELLY: His career was unfortunately ended by injury after he had moved from Leicester to Wolves, but he showed great character in training as a journalist and then, after a spell at the *Express & Star*, he rejoined Wolves as a youth coach. I thoroughly enjoyed travelling with him on scouting missions and his excellent rapport with young players saw him move to a top coaching job with Blackburn Rovers, from where he moved to Leicester City as assistant manager. For me he was a sad loss to Wolves.

MIKE McINDOE: I first saw him playing for Luton reserves and I was grateful to his agent Lorraine Gates for bringing him to my notice again in 2001 when he was available on a free transfer. His immaculate left foot saw him go from strength to strength and, after a spell with Yeovil, he is now with Doncaster in the newly labelled League 1.

ROY McFARLAND: A former England defender who was assistant manager of Derby County when I first moved there. At first I was in awe of him but we became friends, confidants and occasionally travelling companions, and I was flattered when he commended me for some of the new signings I made for his Central League side.

He was always complaining light-heartedly that I was finding forwards rather than defenders, as this would unbalance the side.

DAVE MACKAY: A former captain of Tottenham, Derby and Scotland, Dave had a tremendous presence both as captain and manager. His head tennis sessions at Walsall and elsewhere were legendary and wherever he went he seemed to transform the whole situation. On arrival at Walsall he quickly exchanged the office he had been allocated for one three times as big and made it very comfortable. A truly big football man in every sense of the word and one of the most respected.

NEIL MARTIN: Unheralded and unsung, this former Scottish international did great work among Walsall's younger players in the early 1980s. A firm disciplinarian, he fostered the ideals of hard work and the will to win. Sadly he moved out of the area, but he was a good friend to me during difficult times at Walsall.

GEOFF MORRIS: A diminutive winger who, in his teenage years, seemed destined to become one of the best young players I had ever seen in this area. He had a sweet left foot and became the youngest player up to then to play in Walsall's first team, but asthma unfortunately prevented him from reaching the very top.

KENNY MOWER: Another player with an excellent left foot, Kenny hailed from Bloxwich and I first saw him as a young defender playing in a game at Hampstead in the worst storm I have ever experienced. He went on to play 494 games for Walsall and when he was in the same side as David Preece, Craig Shakespeare and Paul Waddington I have never known the club so well served by left-sided players.

KEITH PEARSON: He became Wolves' secretary after first serving them as accountant. I felt that his contribution to the club was underestimated and that he left rather prematurely. He went on to give equally good service to Derby County and is still a close friend.

NIGEL PEARSON: Nigel is a fine example of how lady luck plays a part in one being in the right place at the right time. I just happened to be watching a game between seventeen and eighteen-year olds in the Peak District when I noticed this tall, commanding centre half. Nigel went on to play splendidly for Shrewsbury in their days in the old Second Division, moved to Sheffield Wednesday for a huge fee and at the time of writing is assistant manager of West Brom. He is one of the most likeable and well-presented football personalities that I have met.

GARY PENDREY: The ideal number two when it comes to management. After a long and successful playing career as a Birmingham City defender, he immediately made an impact as a coach with his bright, breezy personality whatever the weather and whatever the situation, and an asset to any dressing room. He was a sound, supportive friend to me when I was with Wolves and I still have regular contact with this inspirational character.

DAVE PENNEY: I was again lucky to be in the right place at the right time when I saw him playing for Pontefract Colliery in a game at Heanor. One could not miss this lively striker with an eye for goal. And I certainly didn't. Soon he had signed for Derby County and became a regular remember of Roy McFarland's successful Central League team (yes, another striker). After a successful Football League career with Oxford and Swansea he has done well in both coaching and management and has taken Doncaster to successive promotions to land them in the new League 1.

DAVID PREECE: A Shropshire lad who became the epitome of the busy little midfielder with a good left foot, good skill, a good motor and good vision. He starred in Walsall's 1984 win at Arsenal and draw at Liverpool. He won an England 'B' cap in his Luton days and later was assistant to Roy McFarland at both Cambridge and Torquay before returning to his native Shropshire for a spell as Telford coach.

MARK REES: Another local lad who came to Walsall as a schoolboy after being turned down at Villa Park. I signed him the day after and he went on to become a match-winner with his tremendous pace, which on a memorable night at Anfield in February 1984 shook Liverpool in a 2-2 draw. Like good wine, he has matured as a personality as he has got older.

ALLY ROBERTSON: After seventeen seasons with West Bromwich Albion he gave invaluable service to Wolves in the course of over 100 games for them. A dour but lovable Scotsman, he would sweat blood for his team. He was an excellent captain, leading from the front. He could be relied upon to produce the goods himself and also to get the best out of others. He was inspirational in Wolves' rise from the Fourth Division to the Second Division, popular with fans and team-mates alike.

JOHN RUDGE: I remember him as a schoolboy playing for Wolverhampton Schools. A very knowledgeable player and manager, John has become a good friend over the years and in our telephone conversations we have bounced many ideas off each other.

CRAIG SHAKESPEARE: One of a number of young Midlanders who joined Walsall straight from school. One of the successful Walsall youth side under Neil Martin and later a member of their 1984 Milk Cup semi-final team. His powerful left foot brought him 86 goals from midfield at a rate of one every four games.

JOHN SNAPE: An excellent non-League captain with Halesowen, Hereford and Worcester. A hard worker both on and off the field, John was a competitor who never knew when he was beaten. Though a part-time player, he was more of a professional than many full-timers. At the time of writing he is coach to Worcester City. Leadership on the field is something I have always noticed at whatever level and I consider him to be the best non-League captain I have seen. He enjoys his football and it shows.

MALCOLM STARKEY: A successful Shrewsbury player who became a successful secretary with the same club. I always found him to be helpful, supportive and informative. He is a Shrewsbury man to the heart and, having retired as secretary, is still on the board.

COLIN TAYLOR: What can I say about my first professional signing? He was my first claim to fame with his magnificent left foot. If only I could sign someone like him once a month, or even once a season, or even once again. Sadly I attended Colin's funeral in 2005 after his untimely death at the age of 64. Not surprisingly, the service was relayed to many who stood outside the packed crematorium.

GRAHAM TURNER: As a player Graham was the complete professional; conscientious, consistent and scrupulously fair. He carried these qualities into his coaching and management. It was a privilege to work with him for three different clubs over a period of almost twenty years. Graham has earned respect by his honesty and integrity and has been well liked by players and fans alike. He and I, right from the start, had an harmonious working relationship, looking for players who would be a credit to the club. Over the years my family and Graham's family have become friends. I shall never forget Graham regularly visiting me when I was in hospital and providing transport for me when I came out. I was very grateful when he agreed to provide the foreword to this book.

ROY WHALLEY: I knew him as a great Walsall fan when I was there. In 1986 he gave up a teaching career to become a highly successful secretary, commercial manager and director and has enjoyed tremendous success in Walsall's off-field activities, such as Sportsmen's Evenings and the Sunday market at the new Bescot ground.

BERT WILLIAMS: As a goalkeeper he was one of my boyhood heroes at Walsall before he went on to become one of the worlds greatest 'keepers with Wolves and England. Later I had regular contact with him at his goalkeepers' school at Bilston. Then, in my Wolves days, he regularly came into my office and reminisced. A wonderful family man and modest personality, Bert has always been a credit to the game.

BERNIE WRIGHT: I'll never forget the way Bernie looked for my credentials when I first tried to sign him. As a striker he showed total commitment and was a great crowd-pleaser.

# INDEX

# Other titles published by Tempus

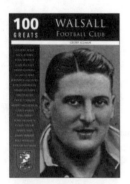

## Walsall Football Club 100 Greats
GEOFF ALLMAN

Walsall have some fine players and these men follow in the footsteps of many others who, in good times and difficult times, have played their hearts out and worn the Walsall FC shirt with pride. This book recalls 100 of those great players, including recent names such as Jimmy Walker and Jorge Leitao, as well as names from the early days at the end of the nineteenth century, such as Sammy Holmes, and characters from all eras in between.

0 7524 2226 X

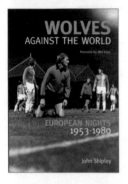

## Wolves Against The World
JOHN SHIPLEY

This unique history of Wolverhampton Wanderers tells the story of the memorable floodlit friendly games in the 1950s, when Wolves took on the very best teams from Europe and the rest of the world, as well as the classic encounters in the European Champions' Cup and European Cup Winners' Cup. Then in the 1960s, '70s and '80s it was the turn of the UEFA Cup, Anglo-Italian Cup and Texaco Cup. This book is bound to evoke wonderful memories for Wolves fans everywhere.

0 7524 2947 7

## Hereford United Football Club 50 Greats
DENISE POWELL & DAVID EDGE

The Edgar Street turf has been graced by some great players since the formation of Hereford United Football Club in 1924. All-time greats such as John Charles, Charlie Thompson, Mel Pejic, Dixie McNeil and Terry Paine will spring to the minds of most supporters, as would the members of the famous giant-killing team. Long-serving members of the current squad take their rightful place in the line-up and some of the new, talented additions to the club have made it into the list.

0 7524 3607 4

## Forever England A History of the National Side
MARK SHAOUL & TONY WILLIAMSON

The definitive history of the English national side. From the days of the amateur gentlemen of the 1870s to the present day, *Forever England* is an insightful and fascinating account of the history of the country's national football team, and covers the careers of England's all-time greats and is an essential read for everyone who is interested in the history of the Three Lions.

0 7524 2939 6

If you are interested in purchasing other books published by Tempus, or in case you have difficulty finding any Tempus books in your local bookshop, you can also place orders directly through our website

**www.tempus-publishing.com**